"**ART** *is the spearhead of human development, social and individual. The vulgarization of art is the surest symptom of ethnic decline.*"

"**SCIENCE** *is not likely to beget a culture unless, and until, a truly universal artistic imagination catches fire from its torch and serves without deliberate intent to give shape to a new feeling, such as generally initiates a new epoch of society.*"

"*Our technological civilization seems to overtake and overwhelm us . . . it makes all our traditional institutions seem inadequate, so that we tend to abandon them.*"

Provocative and profound, Susanne K. Langer's inquiry into the nature of mind and feeling gives us a redefinition of symbol and symbolic thought. Using her characteristic method, the principle of linguistic analysis, she shows that subjective reality cannot be truly reflected in ordinary, discursive language. The primary function of art must be to objectify feelings so that we can contemplate and understand them. With this latest work, Dr. Langer makes clear once more that the function of a philosopher is to scrutinize and define every aspect of the human experience, to strike a generative spark.

MENTOR BOOKS OF RELATED INTEREST

Susanne K. Langer

PHILOSOPHICAL SKETCHES

A MENTOR BOOK PUBLISHED BY
THE NEW AMERICAN LIBRARY

To my sister
ILSE K. DUNBAR
Student of nature, musician, and my truest friend

© 1962, THE JOHNS HOPKINS PRESS,
BALTIMORE, MARYLAND 21233

*Published as a MENTOR BOOK
by arrangement with The Johns Hopkins Press,
who have authorized this softcover edition.
A hardcover edition is available from The Johns Hopkins Press.*

FIRST PRINTING, MAY, 1964

MENTOR TRADEMARK REG. U.S. PAT. OFF. AND FOREIGN COUNTRIES
REGISTERED TRADEMARK—MARCA REGISTRADA
HECHO EN CHICAGO, U.S.A.

MENTOR BOOKS are published *in the United States* by
The New American Library of World Literature, Inc.,
501 Madison Avenue, New York, New York, 10022,
in Canada by The New American Library of Canada Limited,
156 Front Street West, Toronto 1, Ontario,
in the United Kingdom by The New English Library Limited,
Barnard's Inn, Holborn, London, E. C. 1, England

PRINTED IN THE UNITED STATES OF AMERICA

PREFACE

THE ESSAYS AND talks collected in this volume range over many subjects, from quite theoretical ones, such as the paper "On a New Definition of 'Symbol,' " to broad speculations about humanity and its problems—"Man and Animal: The City and the Hive," "The Ultimate Unit," and "The Growing Center of Knowledge." A reader sensitive to style will undoubtedly note, without having to be told, that these papers were addressed to very diverse audiences or presumed readers. The accompanying notes will bear him out. Speaking to the Philosophy Department at Brown University or the Department of Speech at the University of Pittsburgh is, of course, a very different matter from addressing a heterogeneous New York public at Cooper Union. So the language, and the conceptual level, too, have to range from those proper in academic discourse to the popular language and imagery of serious but less-tutored thought.

What conjoins these many topics, however, and prompted their publication in a book, is that they are all studies toward a single much larger work, a philosophy of mind; hence the title, *Philosophical Sketches*. They are previews or incidental products of an undertaking, still in progress, which will require some years for its completion; and they are related to it much as a painter's preliminary pencil or charcoal drawings, or cartoons in large outline, are related to a major oil painting or fresco.

The process of writing such a book as these fragments merely foreshadow is always full of surprises—some welcome, unexpected corroborations or exhibits clinching a doubtful theory, others disconcerting, changing one's ideas in mid-career. In the latter case, what seemed a sure preview only to be elaborated in its final presentation may be altered beyond recognition by deeper study. But freedom to change one's mind is a cardinal aspect of freedom of thought. It is part of that inward freedom which is even more important than any outward liberty to speak one's mind. I am taking that outward liberty largely in order to submit some of the main ideas to criticism that may prove salutary, not only by chastening an overadventurous mind, but especially by offering solutions which long preoccupation with a difficult problem sometimes obscures. The thinker too deeply immersed in the difficulties of, say, symbolism, or individuation, or evolutionary processes, may miss the most obvious implications just because the whole subject has bogged down on its complexities and nothing simple seems plausible any more. Yet a simplification of the problem is often the way to solution, and someone else is more likely to find it than oneself. And there is, furthermore, another motive which induces me to stop in the midst of a long research project and to publish these tentative results: the entirely solitary worker loses touch with the movements of thought and even the subtle development of language in his own profession. It is necessary to set forth one's ideas every so often, lest they become precious "truths" fully understood only by their author— fetishes of an idiosyncratic mind.

On the other hand, there is a real danger in publishing unfinished work, the danger of untimely destructive criticism which can nip it in the bud. All too many readers approach a new theory in the spirit instilled and cultivated by the debating society of their school or college days—the forensic spirit that treats every expositor of ideas as an opponent and seeks, above all, to refute whatever he says, and if possible make it appear as utter nonsense. The chance that the key ideas of any professional scholar's work are pure nonsense is small; much greater the chance that a devastating refutation is based on a superficial reading or even a distorted one, subconsciously twisted by the desire to refute. To attack an error is one thing; to throw out a whole theoretical speculation because it contains an error is another. A serious attack on a fallacious development may set it right, if that is the critic's ambition. Such criticism is co-operative and aims at truth; and it steers its course by checking with the proponent: "Is this what you mean? Is that really what you would say?"

Such caution is particularly necessary in dealing with work that is only briefly stated, i.e., outlined or summarized in a single lecture or article, and especially with hypothetical propositions treated in isolation when their full credentials rest on a larger theoretical foundation. The lack of that systematic construction in a book of anticipatory sketches may indeed be more than what communications engineers call "tolerable perceptual loss"; but if the critic will bear with this shortcoming, and not condemn as unfounded whatever seems to move too freely in intellectual Outer Space, his comments may save the author many a frustration by giving incipient thoughts their turn toward truth before they have grown too rigid to be saved.

S. K. L.

November, 1961

CONTENTS

1 THE PROCESS OF FEELING

AMONG ALL THE facts with which psychologists deal, the
one they seem least able to handle is the fact that we
feel our own activity and the impingements of the world
around us. The metaphysical status of "feelings," "contents of consciousness," "subjectivity," or of the private
aspects of experience generally, has been an asses' bridge
to philosophers ever since Descartes treated *res extensa*
and *res cogitans* as irreducible and incommensurable sub-
stances. The physical scientists have not encountered
this dilemma because their entire interest lies in physical
phenomena, *res extensa;* but the psychologists' proper
interest is really in mental phenomena, which are traditionally ascribed to a nonphysical "order"—mind, consciousness, experience, or what not—some kind of *res
cogitans*.

There is no a priori reason to believe that mental
phenomena constitute any single systematic order, or
that *res extensa* is in essence *non cogitans*. Physical properties are not incompatible with such properties as sensibility and emotivity. But the mutual exclusiveness of
mind and body, active spirit and passive matter, is such
a venerable assumption, rooted so deeply and intricately
in religion and early philosophy, that it seems ineluctable
just by virtue of its long familiarity. To many philosophers and almost all other people it is a deliverance of
common sense. Carl Stumpf declared that it was simply
a fact of nature which no philosophy could circumvent:
"In this respect," he said, "neither Spinoza nor any of
his successors has really transcended the dualism of
Descartes. The truth is that the factual material with

which we are presented shows this double aspect from the very beginning [*schon in der Wurzel*], and . . . *this* duality is impossible to remove." [1] Other psychologists have sought to explain away the "mind-and-body problem" by treating the mind as an "epiphenomenon," produced by the physical changes accessible to science, but falling outside the physical system and therefore not itself an object for scientific research; still others, from Münsterberg [2] at the beginning of our century to Szasz in 1957, [3] have laid the difficulty to a semantic dualism, the existence of a physical vocabulary and an incompatible but equally valid psychological vocabulary that create, respectively, a physical and a psychical version of experience. Which one we choose to employ is a matter of our convenience, but we cannot waver between them without raising the embarrassing issue of brain versus mind. The most respectable position today is, of course, that of the behaviorists: the programmatic refusal to accept anything but overt behavior as a psychological datum, or to treat behavior as an indication that anything is felt by the subject. Some behaviorists have gone so far as to deny the existence of inward experience; others only proscribe the mention of it in their science, and relegate the question of its existence to metaphysics, by which they understand (or rather, misunderstand) some kind of fanciful natural history deduced from the postulates of traditional ethics and religion. In this belief they are fortified by some eminent philosophers, such as Santayana who wrote: "Metaphysics, in the proper sense of the word, is dialectical physics, or an attempt to determine matters of fact by means of logical or moral or rhetorical constructions." [4]

Behaviorism of some sort and degree has become such a prevailing attitude today in psychology, sociology, and various related fields of study that these are generally

---

[1] Abh. d. Königl.-preuss. Akad. d Wissensch. IV (1906), p. 14.

[2] E.g., *Science and Idealism*, 1906.

[3] Thomas S. Szasz, *Pain and Pleasure. A Study of Bodily Feelings.* N.Y., 1957.

[4] From the preface to *Skepticism and Animal Faith;* quoted by Irwin Edman, *The Philosophy of George Santayana* (New York, 1936), p. 370.

called "the behavioral sciences." Yet the term is not simply descriptive; it expresses a methodology and, further, an accepted belief about the relation of metaphysics to those sciences, if not about metaphysics itself. The consensus of social scientists, especially in America, is that such a metaphysical problem as the existence of something called "feeling," "consciousness," or "subjective experience" lies outside the realm of factual description which is the realm of science, and that consequently one may hold any philosophical opinion on such matters without the least effect on one's scientific investigations and findings.

This opinion seems to me to be erroneous. The sciences are really born of philosophy; they do not simply arise from controlled observation when philosophy is finally slain and cleared away to permit their growth. They are born under quite special conditions—when their key concepts reach a degree of abstraction and precision which makes them adequate to the demands of exact, powerful, and microscopically analytic thinking. Philosophy is the formulation and logical exploration of concepts. Therefore it is a philosophical event that generates a young, exciting, it may be blundering, science—the reconception of facts under a new abstractive principle, in a new intellectual projection. Newton's concept of gravity as a property of matter was such a concept; so was the concept of evolution which Darwin's *Origin of Species* sprang upon the world (though he was not its sole originator), to transform the whole study of natural history from pure taxonomy into a science of biology. But the greatest of all philosophical insights, the first generative idea begetting any science at all, lies near the beginning of our whole intellectual culture—the concept of transformation of matter, which we meet first in the physical doctrines of the early Ionians. It has become such a basic assumption in our scientific thought, and has been so highly corroborated by experience, that we no longer recognize it as a philosophical notion. We have extended it from "matter" to "energy" and all other conceptions of physical reality. But it really was a bold metaphysical conception; some of Thales' contemporaries could still say, "The sun is new every day."

The frustrating situation which prevents a vigorous advance in modern psychology is that it cannot deal conceptually with its own essential subject matter—mental phenomena. Its methods are all evasion and circumvention of traditional terms and the untenable assumptions those terms express. But no amount of criticism, avoidance, and safeguarding against false ideas can give the study of mind what it needs for its own development into a science—a tenable idea strong enough to give negotiable meanings to such terms as "subjective," "felt," "conscious," "mental," and the topic itself that it purports to deal with—mind. Its present key concepts are neither abstract enough nor capable of the high elaboration a real natural science calls for. "Behavior," "stimulus," and "response" are working notions of the animal laboratory, generalized and stretched in the hope of covering the whole field of psychological facts; but beyond the context in which they were originated—experimentation on animals—they quickly decline in usefulness. A term that *designates* a vast variety of phenomena cannot be used to describe their differences, let alone to account for them. Abstractions do not designate phenomena at all, but serve to describe them. There is no object or event called "gravity," but such phenomena as the flow of water downhill, the position of stars in relation to each other, the attraction of a compass needle to the magnetic pole, are widely diverse events or conditions describable by use of the concept of gravity. There are such things as stimuli and responses; to isolate and label them, even to pair some very simple ones, is a sort of taxonomy; it does not furnish any principles of analysis or construction, any terms to describe the relations between observed events.

Psychology, which is no longer as young as its apologists like to consider it, does not grow apace with other new sciences, for instance biology, because its conceptual framework is too weak to allow the heavy strains of bold speculative hypothesis to be laid on it. The psychologist is not free to use his scientific imagination because the edges of his field are carefully staked out and blocked with warnings against the quagmires and pitfalls of wrong "isms." Those edges have to be cleared before any edifice of science can be built that may ultimately demand great space.

Several attempts have been made to redefine "mind" and "mental" in some scientifically safe and yet adequate way. Able thinkers like Bertrand Russell and Gilbert Ryle have undertaken such redefinitions,[5] but for some reason the results have done nothing to promote or facilitate research, or suggest a new approach to basic problems. That reason is, I think, that both Lord Russell and Mr. Ryle hold with the positivists and most behaviorists that metaphysical issue should be left alone. The general conviction of those schools is that metaphysical ideas are irrelevant to science, since they apply to the universe as a whole, about which nothing can really be known. But the truth is, I think, that all scientific analyses when pursued far enough go down to implicit metaphysical propositions, which need not be about the universe as a whole, but about the nature of things in it. Whitehead once defined metaphysics as "the most general statements we can make about reality." Whether we make them or not, their content is assumed in less general assertions, because they embody our basic concepts; and if these do not fit whatever aspects or items of reality we are talking about, we raise insoluble problems, as in unpurified psychological theory.

The intellectual timidity that inhibits our theoretical thinking in psychology springs from an unresolved philosophical problem, metaphysical if you like, a basic misconception; and the way to remove that incubus is not to sidle past it with averted gaze, but to face and tackle it. I doubt, furthermore, that a redefinition of "mind" is an immediate need for our thinking about mind, any more than a perfectly satisfactory definition of "matter" was ever needed to beget physics. A definition of the subject matter itself—in psychology, "mind"—is the ultimate aim of scientific theory, and at best may be expected to emerge when the theory reaches a high degree of applicability and speculative power. What is needed

---

[5] Bertrand Russell, *The Analysis of Mind* (London and New York, 1921); Gilbert Ryle, *The Concept of Mind* (New York, 1949). See also Charles W. Morris, *Six Theories of Mind* (Chicago, 1932).

at the beginning is an adequate definition of working concepts, in terms of which our knowledge of "matter," "mind," "life," or whatever may be the whole field of inquiry, is to be handled.

As I remarked at the outset, the greatest bugbear to psychology is the fact that most creatures—the higher animals, certainly—are sentient, that this is really what distinguishes them from inanimate mechanisms, however elaborate, and even from such animate ones as plants, which probably do not feel the influences controlling their lives, or their own responses. The subject matter of psychology was originally staked out by that differentia; and an impasse which forces a science to eschew its real subject matter because it cannot be scientifically handled points to a basic misconception, some tacit metaphysical assumption that is wrong.

The misconception leading us into sterile theories of mind is the notion of feeling as a separate sort of entity, ontologically distinct from physical entities and therefore belonging to a different order or constituting a different "realm." I am using the word "feeling" not in the arbitrarily limited sense of "pleasure or displeasure" to which psychologists have often restricted it, but on the contrary in its widest possible sense, i.e., to designate *anything that may be felt.* In this sense it includes both sensation and emotion—the felt responses of our sense organs to the environment, of our proprioceptive mechanisms to internal changes, and of the organism as a whole to its situation as a whole, the so-called "emotive feelings." We feel warmth, pinprick, ache, effort, and relaxation; vision is the way the optic apparatus feels the impingement of light, and hearing is the way the auditory structures feel sound waves; we feel bodily weakness or high tonus, and we feel expectation, frustration, yearning, fear, satisfaction. All these ways of feeling have characteristic forms, and a closer study of their forms shows a striking resemblance between them and the forms of growth, motion, development, and decline familiar to the biologist, the typical forms of vital process. This suggests a more intimate relation between such process and the phenomenon of sentience than their traditional treatment as categorically separate sets of "data" would ever suggest. The very notion of "data" tends subtly to break up the "given" into so many entities; and the peculiar trick of our language which lets us say either, "I feel thus and thus," or "I have such and such a feeling," and regard these two expressions as equivalent, serves and fixes the hypostatization. So we look for some systematic connection between entities of two incongruous kinds, physical and psychical—nerve tissue and sensation, brain and mind.

The psychological fact, however, is that an organism feels something; to feel is an activity, not a product. It is something that goes on in the organism, but not necessarily an isolable event over and above those which we are gradually and indirectly observing, the actions of the brain and its dependencies.

The hypothesis—and it is, of course, nothing more—which I have found rewarding beyond expectation is that sentience is a phase of vital process itself, a strictly intraorganic phase, i.e., an appearance which is presented only within the organism in which the activity occurs. Each organism, therefore, feels its own actions if they enter this phase, and not any other creature's. Not many of the myriad events that make up a life are felt at all—probably only those of unusual intensity. Such intense physiological action requires very complex integrated functions, and is therefore likely to be limited to the highest, most elaborated anatomical structures. Probably it always involves some nervous tissue; perhaps it occurs only in that most energized organic substance. That is a problem which only direct or indirect experimental research can solve. When the activity of some part of the nervous system reaches a critical pitch, the process is felt; this is a characteristic vital phenomenon, though by no means ubiquitous. The amount of internal action and even "behavior" that may occur below the limen of sentience is often surprising. A felt process is felt in the organ wherein it occurs; one may say that the process has gone into *psychical phase*.[6]

---

[6] The word "psychical" is used somewhat differently by psychoanalysts, especially C. G. Jung and his disciples, who mean by it what I would rather call "cerebral functions," felt or unfelt. But any word one could prefer would be equally pre-empted for spe-

All sorts of new possibilities of analysis and inquiry are brought into speculative and even experimental reach by regarding feeling as part and parcel of vital action instead of as a "nonmaterial" product of such action, or, worse yet for science, as an "epiphenomenal correlate" of physical processes.[7] For one thing, this hypothesis resolves the problem posed and found insoluble by the great neurologist, Wilder Penfield, when he said: "It is obvious that nerve impulse is somehow converted into thought and that thought can be converted into nerve impulse. And yet this all throws no light on the nature of that strange conversion." [8] If, instead of "converted into thought," we say, "felt as thought," the investigation of mental function is shifted from the realm of mysterious transubstantiation to that of physiological processes, where we face problems of complexity and degree, which are difficult, but not unassailable in principle.

The expression "felt as thought," which is here substituted for "converted into thought," raises another issue, the power of a new concept to concatenate the findings in a general field of research. "Feeling" in the broad sense here employed seems to be the generic basis of all mental experience—sensation, emotion, imagination, recollection, and reasoning, to mention only the main categories. *Felt experience* is elaborated in the course of high organic development, intellectualized as brain functions are corticalized, and socialized with the evolution of speech and the growth of its communicative functions.[9] On the other hand, the mechanisms of felt activity are heightened forms of unfelt vital rhythms, responses, and interactions; a psychology oriented by this concept of feeling runs smoothly downward into physiology without the danger of being reduced to physiology

---

cial uses; so the reader must be requested to recognize a special use here.

[7] This old double-entry psychology has given way to the current double-aspect view, which sees the connection between objective physical events and subjective experiences as a semantic shift from one "logical language" to another.

[8] "Some Observations on the Functional Organization of the Human Brain," *Proc. Am. Philos. Soc.*, XCVIII (1954), 293–97; see p. 297.

[9] Cf. "Speculations on the Origins of Speech and Its Communicative Functions" (No. 2, below).

and therewith losing its own identity. Even if it should ultimately appear as a branch of physiology, the area of its branching is likely to remain quite visible, though without a sharp dividing line (there are very few such sharp lines in nature): it is the area where vital (probably neural) processes begin to have psychical phases, i.e., to be felt. We may not always be able to judge what activities are felt; such judgments, with respect to speechless creatures, rest on many speculative grounds, not only analogies between animal and human behavior, but especially phylogenetic continuities and structural homologies.

Feeling, as we all know, is divided almost from the outset into two general categories, which may be called sensibility and emotivity. Some very interesting work has been done on the problem of this division, especially by psychologists who postulate an original undifferentiated *Gemeingefühl* in which sensation and emotive response are not yet distinguishable.[10] Perhaps the differentiation of these two orders goes further back than any other, as the difference between the neural actions at the periphery of the organism and in its spinocerebral structures very generally does. The periphery, which both exploits and resists the surrounding world, is organized for constant emergencies; its innervation is characterized by quick and selective responses to stimuli that evoke reactions without preparation. The central responses are slower and somewhat massive; the organism as a whole prepares itself and goes into action with gathering force, be it fast or slow. This difference carries through even to the psychical level of the respective actions: outside stimulations are felt as impacts, unprepared events, that the organism ordinarily copes with in its course, but may also meet defensively if they are violent, as it meets

---

[10] See, for instance, the many works of Heinz Werner, which deal with interrelations among the several special senses too, and between perception and movement; esp. *Entwicklungspsychologie* (Leipzig, 1933); "Motion and Motion Perception: a Study in Vicarious Functioning," *J. Psychol.*, XIX (1945), 317–27. See also H. Werner and S. Wapner, "Toward a General Theory of Perception," *Psychol. Rev.*, LIX (1952), 324–38; Hans Hoff, "Beiträge zur Relation der Sehsphäre und des Vestibulapparates," *Ztschr. f. ges. Neurol. u. Psychiat.*, CXXI (1929), 751–62.

loud noises, excessive light, and injurious contacts. The activities that rise to feeling within the central nervous system are usually less abrupt and betray no definite point of origin; they feel like autogenic actions rather than impingements. Briefly, one may say that peripherally started nervous excitations are normally though not always *felt as impact,* centrally started ones *felt as action.*

This distinction is of great psychological importance, especially its abnormalities, which often point the investigator to unsuspected, far-reaching aspects of mental life. It also permits some very useful definitions of terms, which come into play with the development of basic problems of individuation, participation, sensory projection, expressive functions, and social involvement—that is, problems from the most elementary to the most advanced stages of systematic inquiry—notably, the terms *subjective* and *objective.* We experience as objective whatever is felt as impact, and as subjective what is felt as action. The use of these definitions invites one to recognize many intriguing, usually overlooked phenomena, such as the dialectical interplay between subjective and objective elements in human experience, the lability of these characters themselves, the points of their disappearance or possibly even their reversal; one is led to problems of objectification, which are crucial in the psychology of art and indeed of all symbolic behavior.

The greatest advantage, however, to be gained from the conception of feeling as a phase of living process itself, instead of as a product or "psychical correlate" of it, is that it contains implicitly the solution of the moot problems of "consciousness" and "the unconscious." There are *conscious acts,* which may be widely or narrowly defined according to the context in which the word is used; and there is such a thing as *consciousness,* the general mode or degree of feeling which marks a creature's mental activities as a whole at a given time, and which may vary under conditions that affect all acts in psychical phase together, as, for instance, intoxicants, opiates, and other chemicals do. Then we may properly speak of "alterations of consciousness." But there is no "realm" or "system" of consciousness, which contains "ideas" in the sense of Locke and his successors, no "contents of consciousness" or things "given to consciousness." These deceptive figures of speech have become so ensconced in our professional idiom that they look innocent, and writers who explicitly reject the notion of "consciousness" as a receptacle or any sort of entity will often fall back, in the very same discourse, into the old forms of thought they have just repudiated. As long as no alternative concept has really filled the place of those discarded hypostatizations they are still dogging our imagination and have to be repulsed again and again. The best guarantee of an adequate conceptual formulation is that it suddenly does away with what may seem like a purely literary temptation, the constant temptation to use metaphors and stock phrases which embody obsolete theories.[11]

As for "the unconscious," it is simply not needed once we treat feeling as a phase of processes which in most of their stages are not felt. The conception of "ideas" stored in "the unconsciousness" is an inheritance from earlier theories of mind. According to the view here proposed, a great deal of cerebration goes on below the limen of feeling, and many activities play across it so that they barely and briefly, though perhaps repeatedly, rise above it. Yet they interact with others which have strong and specialized psychical character, and their influence is reflected in those conscious processes; the entirely unfelt ones comprise most of the work for which Freud postulated a special agency, "the unconscious system." They probably do not compose a system, but are part and parcel of the extensive functions that be-

[11] This tendency is still strongly marked in scientific works on evolution and the broader aspects of biology generally, often by the most competent thinkers, who certainly would not subscribe to any literal meaning of their inherited language. "Nature's plans," "nature's experiments," "her" acts of selection and care for species survival have replaced the older language of God's wisdom and power, but the familiar metaphors are still the readiest expressions, which means that they still fall in with a disavowed habit of thinking in teleological terms of providence and final causation. Scientists may take such language as mere stylistic ornament, but for the layman it becomes practically impossible to abandon his mythical mode of thought if the scientific literature itself preserves its forms for him.

long essentially to the central nervous system, with its highest activity in the brain.

The specializations of sensibility, as so many special senses, have been fairly widely studied; less so, the articulations of what may, by way of distinction, be called "emotivity" into specialized processes, such as image formation (under the influence of sensory impressions), subjectification and the whole gamut of emotions, objectification and symbolic projection, and with the advent (apparently not below the human level) of symbol-making and symbol-using functions, the highly articulated processes of discursive thought. As soon as one ventures at all boldly and seriously into such territory, the problems that invite research lead in every direction and appear staggered one behind another. But there are lines of order among them, and certainly different degrees of amenability: sometimes indirect methods are furnished by neurological or psychiatric study, or suggested by theories evolved in other quarters as diverse as chemistry, small-current engineering, and (no less important) the philosophy of art and of language.

All investigations of mental phenomena are difficult if they are pursued to any extent and in serious fashion. There is no reason why the most intricate, sensitive, and versatile structures in nature, organisms controlled by elaborate nervous systems, should be easier to understand than the structures that confront the physicist, or why a psychologist should be content with recording and co-ordinating crude molar observations and stating their most obvious regularities as "laws." The fast-growing complexity and theoretical challenge of problems are healthy signs that a real science is in the making. As soon as we can conceive a continuity of physical sensitivity and felt impression, physical action and mentation, we have all biological findings and their implications to build on. We can search for the foundations of feeling as far back in phylogenetics as our ingenuity will take us, and not be afraid that too much physiological explanation will make us "merely physiologists" instead of psychologists—any more than a physiologist has to take care lest his advance to more and more chemical explanations may make him "merely a chemist."

As vigorously as a conceptually clear construction of mental life sends its roots downward into more general knowledge of life as such, genuinely psychological problems grow up and branch out one from another. What sort of process is image formation? How and to what extent is the visual apparatus—from the eyes to the farthest reaches of the visual radiation, probably beyond the striate area—involved in it? Is it the essential mechanism of fantasy, or only a contributive factor? Is it likely to be developed in animal brains? What evidence could one seek—analogous electroencephalographic results,[12] or, in animals, trustworthy behavioral signs of hallucination in febrile or toxic states, comparable to conditions we know experientially? The door is wide open for ingenious research methods. And furthermore, wherever in the evolutionary scale imagery first occurs (one might hesitate to attribute it to reptiles or fish), what cerebral developments or pressures bring it about? Does it always serve the purposes it serves in human brains? What are its connections with emotions on the one hand, and on the other with the progressive intellectualization of mental acts in man?

Answers to such questions are devious, and can seldom be found singly. As a theory evolves it raises problems which can be tackled only in its own advancing context, on a basis of previously decided issues. But the concept of feeling here proposed lends itself to a fairly precise construction of many terms that are ordinarily used in loose fashion or evaded because of their looseness, but that could and should be available for exact thinking—terms like "mental," "psychosomatic," "voluntary," "potential," or like "projection," "tendency," "aim." Other key concepts needed for the understanding of psychical phenomena lie even further back in the foundations of biology, but the need for them emerges only when the high-level functions properly called "psychological" come under consideration; then such elementary concepts as "act," "dialectic," and "rhythm" have to be construed. Perhaps biology it-

---

[12] Grey Walter has found interesting effects in human experimentation, where the subject can report on his imagery.

self will be led to some theoretical advances by the demands of psychology, as physics grew to meet the problems posed by chemistry when the differences between chemical "elements" were hypothetically laid to atomic structure.

In the compass of a single article one cannot illustrate by examples the building up of philosophical ideas that really promises to culminate in a sound concept of mind, but the work is under way. The best indication of its promise is that each new theoretical construction gives importance and new connectedness to work that has already been done, sometimes quite long ago—detailed work, scattered throughout the medical, psychological, philosophical, and other literature, studies of instinct, of evolutionary change, of "conditioned reflexes," animal perception, learning, and habituation, chemical and physiological studies of endocrine and drug action, of growth induction, emotional effects ("sham" emotion), alterations of consciousness in human beings. There is a wealth of clinical material on motor disturbance from visible cerebral causes and from psychosomatic causes, and especially on such mental aberrations as amnesia, acalculia, agnosia of all sorts; these data cast separate lights on functions usually so integrated in human mentality that their origins are obscured, unless that mentality falls apart and reveals its unsuspected factors. The versatility and interrelatedness of all parts of the central nervous system are unbelievable. Even the special senses, which so far have been studied by psychologists almost entirely with respect to their obvious use as guides for the organism's dealings with the world beyond its skin, have exhibited another capacity in the recent much-publicized experiments on sensory deprivation: our constant sensory stimulation, even without conveying any new information, serves to keep us realistic in waking life to the extent of not letting the brain freely hallucinate as in dream.

The brain with all its extensions is the organ of animal mentality, and it is, of course, an epoch-making development in that organ that raises human mentality to the status properly called "mind." Its critical moment was probably the beginning of symbolic activity; and although we can only speculate on the causes and natural history of that function, it is possible and rewarding to do so. The hypothesis that presents itself from the biological standpoint here taken has some of the marks of fertile theory, in that it presents "mind" as a natural phenomenon, and lets one attack the most intriguing of all psychological problems—the tremendous difference between man and all other creatures—instead of evading or belittling it; and also in that it explains, quite incidentally, why the mind seems so much like a separate entity and independent agent that it has been quite universally regarded as a homunculus, an "inner man" dwelling in the body, giving life and motion to it and leaving it at death.

The basis of these claims is material for a long book and cannot be presented here, let alone discussed. But an indication can perhaps be given of what makes an act "mental," and of how animal mentality may be supposed to have eventuated in the higher form characteristic of man, which we mean by "mind."

The central nervous system seems to develop in the Metazoa just as the various species evolve the "distance receptors" of smell and sight, and at fairly high levels, hearing. It is essentially a mechanism steering the activities of the animal as a whole by more specialized and concentrated cues than the general conditions that attract and repel very primitive creatures; and its simplest form is a system of complementary afferent and efferent nerves, bringing in sensory impressions and sending out corresponding impulses to muscles and other organs (glands, lungs, etc.) to effect appropriate action.

At least a gloss is needed here to stand in for the whole chapter that is really required to define and justify the concept of "action" and its specializations, "activity" and "act." A brief note on the meaning of "act" will have to orient us in the present discussion. An act is a special sort of event, always in an organism.[13] What characterizes it is that it involves a complex of tensions,

---

[13] This statement may have to be modified in such special contexts as those of jurisprudence and ethnology.

either local or affecting the whole organism, but perhaps always with a center of excitement; this whole complex arises as one process and resolves as such, whereupon the act is finished. The modes of rise and resolution vary immensely. Some acts have psychical phases; the great majority occur unfelt.

The most problematical activity of an animal's central nervous system lies between the afferent and efferent conductors, where the perceptual act terminates and the motor act starts in response. In the so-called "reflex arc" which is generally regarded as the prototype of all animal behavior,[14] there is a point of change from reception to reaction; the neural structures which effect this change are highly complex, and tend to specialize more and more. In vertebrates they lie in the spinal cord and the brain, but in the latter organ they are often so elaborated and also complicated by integration with other functional units that reflex acts become minor ingredients in its activity.

Mental acts are acts which center in the brain and are felt—that is, have some psychic phase. There are many cerebral acts which are not mental, though they may modify mental acts;[15] the entire activity imputed to "the unconscious" is of this class. Also, acts which do not center in the brain may be felt, for instance, in creatures which have only diffuse innervation. Such organisms may nevertheless feel the impacts to which they respond, and perhaps their own excitements—we cannot know. Where there is a forebrain there are specialized, presumably mental acts: awareness, intent, emotion, suspense and decision, desire, perhaps gratification. The focusing on a perceived object, e.g., an obstacle, or the goal of a leap or dash, is in all likelihood a mental act. But, be that as it may, in animals the

[14] A reasonable hypothesis, yet perhaps too confidently taken for known fact. Ontogenetically, it seems to be preceded by more complex functions, the prompt "reflex" resulting from simplification with maturation. See R. Lorente de Nó, "Vestibulo-ocular Reflex Arc," *Arch. Neurol. & Psychiat.*, XXX (1933), 245–91.

[15] Acts may expand and incorporate other acts, or be articulated within a general activity and become specialized in character and effect. All such characterizations which are needed to build up the theoretical notion of "act" have to be left unexpounded here.

total response usually enlists the whole body, i.e., the mental element belongs to a greater dynamic pattern; this greater physical act is guided throughout by perception and intention. The animal brain is above all a cybernetic organ controlling the organism's overt responses to the opportunities and obstacles which the environment offers.

In man, nervous sensitivity is so high that to respond with a muscular act to every stimulus of which he takes cognizance would keep him in a perpetual St. Vitus's dance. A great many acts, started in his brain by his constant discriminative perception of sights, sounds, proprioceptive reports, and so on, have no overt phase at all, but are finished in the brain; their conclusion is the formation of an image, the activation of other cell assemblies that run through their own repertoire of word formation or what not, perhaps the whole elaborate process that constitutes an act of ideation. One act starts another; a great proportion of such intracerebral events rise to feeling, and, moreover, they are chiefly felt as action, i.e., they are subjective. At the present stage of our natural history, the human brain seems to be constantly thinking, remembering, recording, or dreaming—most often, in the waking state, all of these together, or in kaleidoscopic successions (in sleep, dream seems to take over almost entirely). The result of this heightened and largely self-perpetuating activity is that we continuously feel our own inward action as a texture of subjectivity, on which such objectively felt events as perceptions impinge, and from which our more sustained and complete subjective acts, such as concerted thought or distinct emotions, stand out as articulate forms. That psychical continuum is our self-awareness; when it is broken, as in some pathological states, no amount of objective evidence can convince the patient that his subjectively "lost" hand, foot, or even half of his body is his own.[16]

---

[16] The literature is too extensive and scattered to list, but some collected case histories and discussions may be found in Paul Schilder, *The Image and Appearance of the Human Body* (New York, 1950), and in J. M. Nielsen, *Agnosia, Apraxia, Aphasia* (New York, 1946).

The completion of peripherally or centrally started acts within the brain usually strikes into other cerebral events; and it may have been an intolerable crowding of impulses that finally led to the most momentous evolutionary step in our phylogenetic past, the rise of a spontaneous symbolic identification of percepts, recollections, and free images or figments with each other, which grew into a characteristic and pervasive tendency. By what actual events and stages this function may have developed is a problem as frightening as it is luring, though perhaps not beyond the bourn of hypothetical construction; but it cannot be broached here. All I can say here is that from a primitive symbolic relation in which symbol and sense are seen as an identity,[17] all the higher forms of symbolic thinking and communication have stemmed, by virtue of which man's mentality, and his alone, is a mind. As his subjective experience is intensified and integrated into a self, his objective experience is symbolically unified into a world; the interplay of these two mental constructs governs his life, which is therefore really a "life of the mind."

This hypothesis, built on the concept of feeling as a characteristic of the most complex and energized vital processes, presents the mind as a hominid specialty, a functional phenomenon resulting from the extraordinary development of man's central nervous system. It also does what a successful hypothesis may be counted on to do—namely, yield some incidental explanations for which it was not expressly intended. One of these is the side light it throws on the peculiar tendency of people in practically all ages and cultures to regard the mind as an entity, a soul inhabiting and using the rest of the organism, which by contrast is "its" body. At the risk of overtaxing the reader's patience I shall

[17] A good deal of evidence for such a phase in symbolic thinking is brought by E. Cassirer in *The Philosophy of Symbolic Forms* (New Haven, Conn., 1953), esp. Vol. II, and in much briefer fashion in his *Language and Myth* (New York, 1945). An astonishingly convergent treatment and almost identical theory, independently developed at the same time, may be found in Owen Barfield, *Poetic Diction: A Study in Meaning* (London, 1928). See also my *Philosophy in a New Key* (Cambridge, Mass., 1942), Chs. 6 and 7.

briefly adduce this one example of such theoretical implications.

The brain is an organ, and like all organs it is built into a greater living whole, an organism, which it helps to sustain by its special functions. If it develops beyond the exact needs of the organism it presents a threat of separate individuation (another fundamental principle that has not even been discussed above) within the individual to which it belongs. Something like this holds for the human brain. It takes up so many stimulations that have to be dealt with mainly in its own systematic way that the need of finishing every started act, which characterizes living tissues, causes it to have interests of its own, beyond the interests of the organism: the needs of symbolization, expression, ideation, logical thought (achieving order among ideas), and especially communication, which absorbs and governs the chaotic emotional activity engendered by thought and fantasy. We have, consequently, a sort of "inner life," or life of the mind, which makes the mind seem like a separate being in the body. Since it obviously also controls the organism as a whole, it is almost inevitably regarded as a governing agent, the whole man's double or soul.

It takes more than one idea, however fertile, to build a science, and generally each new major insight makes the last one obsolete. By the time the study of mind can really take its place among true sciences, the concept of feeling as I have formulated it here will probably appear naïve, not to say quaint. But meanwhile it may still serve the most pressing need of our day, to bring mental phenomena into the compass of natural fact, so that we can scare up and pursue any problem we like without fear of riding for a metaphysical fall.

2 SPECULATIONS ON THE ORIGINS OF SPEECH AND ITS COMMUNICATIVE FUNCTION*

EVER SINCE the Darwinian theory of human evolution —tracing the descent of man from animal ancestors —has become generally accepted, the origin of speech has become more and more mystifying. Language is so much the mark of man that it was classically supposed to have been bestowed on him at his creation. But if he has not been created separately from the animals, but has arisen, as most of us now believe, just as they arose, from a more primitive animal ancestry, then surely at some time his own precursors did not speak. When, why, and how did man begin to speak? What generations invented that great social instrument, language? What development of animal communication has eventuated in human communication? What pre-Adamite thought of assigning a particular little squeak to a particular object as the name of that object, by which you could refer to it, demand it, make other people think of it? How did the other pre-Adamites all agree to assign the same squeaks to the same things? What has led to the concatenation of those primitive words in syntactically structured sentences of interrelated meanings? As far as anthropologists know, there is no human language that is not discursive—propositional—in form. Its propositions may be very different from ours, but their semantic structure is always equivalent to what we call a statement. Language always expresses relations among acts or things, or their aspects. It always makes reference to

* This paper was read at the University of Pittsburgh, under the auspices of the Department of Speech, and published in *The Quarterly Journal of Speech XLVI* (1960), 121–134.

reality—that is, makes assertions or denials—either explicitly or implicitly. Some nouns imply relations, and where they do, verbs may not be needed. In classical Latin the verb is often understood through the inflections of nouns and adjectives. Verbs, in some languages, may imply their subject or object or even both, and make nouns all but unnecessary, as Whorf found in Hopi.[1] But no language consists of signs that only call attention to things without saying anything about them—that is, without asserting or denying something. All languages we know have a fairly stabile vocabulary and a grammatical structure. No language is essentially exclamatory (like ah! and oh!), or emotional (like whining and yodeling), or even imperative.[2] The normal mode of communicative speech, in every human society, is the indicative; and there is no empirical evidence, such as a correlation of increasing discursiveness with increasing culture, to support the belief that it was ever otherwise.

Language may be used to announce one's presence, to greet people, to warn, to threaten, to express pain or joy, or even for directing action.[3] Whenever people speak of "animal language" they refer to such uses of observable signs among animals.[4] Leaving aside, for the moment, the alleged "language" of social insects,[5] we may use the term *vocal signs* among animals.

Now, it is an obvious common-sense assumption that human language has grown from some such lower form

[1] Benjamin Lee Whorf, "Languages and Logic," *Technol. Rev.* XLIII (1941), 270.

[2] Note, however, H. J. Pos, "Réflexions sur le problème de l' origine du langage," *Acta psychol.* (1950), who maintains that the *primary* forms of language were imperative and vocative.

[3] John Dewey, in *Experience and Nature* (Chicago, 1925), p. 175, says that primitive signs "become language only when used within a context of mutual assistance and direction. The latter are alone of prime importance in considering the transformation of organic gestures and cries into names, things with significance, or the origin of language."

[4] See, for example, J. B. S. Haldane, "Animal Communication and the Origin of Human Language," *Science Progress*, CLXXI (1955), 385–401; and esp. Julian Huxley and Ludwig Koch, *Animal Language* (London, 1938).

[5] K. von Frisch, *Bees: Their Vision, Chemical Senses, and Language* (Ithaca, N. Y., 1950); see also *The Dancing Bees* (New York, 1955).

of vocal communication. But common sense is a very tricky instrument; it is as deceptive as it is indispensable. Because we use it, and have to use it, all the time, we tend to trust it beyond its real credentials, and to feel disconcerted if its simple interpretations of experience fail. Yet common-sense conceptions of the nature and origin of human speech have always led into dilemmas, until the problem of its beginning and development has been generally given up.

Even methodology develops its common-sense principles. One of these is that, if you would find the important relationships between two phenomena, you should begin by checking what the phenomena have in common. So, in comparing the vocal communications of animals and men, respectively, we find that all the things animals communicate by sound may also be communicated by human language; and it seems reasonable enough that those things which human language can do and animal vocalization cannot have been added to the primitive animal language, to make the greatly elaborated system of verbal intercourse.[6] But the finding of these common elements leads no further. Common-sense methodology, like the common-sense assumptions, produces nothing more than what we already knew—by common sense.

So it may be in order to question our obvious premises, and even depart from the method of seeking common factors in animal and human communication. Instead of noting points of similarity, let us consider the cardinal difference between human and animal language. That difference is in the *uses* to which utterances are put. All those functions that animal and human utterances share—calling, warning, threatening, expressing emotion—are essential uses of animal sounds, and incidental uses of human speech. The functions of animal vocalization are self-expression and sometimes, perhaps, indication of environmental conditions (like the

---

[6] This is the view expressed by Charles Morris in *The Nature of Mind* (Houston, Texas, 1929), and in *Signs, Language and Behavior* (New York, 1946); also by John Dewey, *op. cit.*, and elsewhere.

bark of a dog who wants to be let in). The chief function of speech is denotation.

Animal language is not language at all, and, what is more important, *it never leads to language*.[7] Dogs that live with men learn to understand many verbal signals, but only as signals, in relation to their own actions. Apes that live in droves and seem to communicate fairly well never *converse*.[8] But a baby that has only half a dozen words begins to converse: "Daddy gone." "Daddy come? Daddy come." Question and answer, assertion and denial, denotation and description—these are the basic uses of language.

The line between animal and human estate is, I think, the language line; and the gap it marks between those two kinds of life is almost as profound as the gap between plants and animals. This makes it plausible that we are not dealing with just a higher form of some general animal function, but with a new function developed in the hominid brain—a function of such complexity that probably not one, but many, subhuman mental activities underlie it.

[7] See L. Boutan, "Le pseudo-langage: observations effectées sur un anthropoide, le gibbon (Hylobates Leucogenys-Obilby)," *Act. Soc. Linnéenne Bordeaux,* LCVII (1913), 5–77; he remarks on the vocal habits of gibbons, "les animaux n'ont pas un langage rudimentaire. Leur langage n' est pas un langage."

[8] See R. M. Yerkes and H. W. Nissen, "Prelinguistic Sign Behavior in the Chimpanzee," *Science,* LXXXIX, n.s. (1939) 585–87. The upshot of the reported experiments is "that delayed response, in the absence of spatial cues or with misleading cues, is either extremely difficult or impossible for most chimpanzees. . . . There is abundant evidence that various other types of sign process than the symbolic are of frequent occurrence and function effectively in the chimpanzee" (p. 587). Perhaps the title *"Non-linguistic Sign Behavior . . ."* would have been more accurate.

Despite such observations, the authors of *Animal Language* do not hesitate to attribute conversation to monkeys, and even to animals below the primates, or to refer to their repertoire of sounds as a vocabulary having direct affinities with human speech. "The gregarious baboons," writes Sir Julian, who composed the text, "are very conversational animals. Most of its communications, both in the pack and in its component family groups, are effected by voice" (Huxley and Koch, *op. cit.,* p. 55). And more remarkable still: "The sea-lions . . . as befits their social and intelligent nature, are noisy animals, and possess a considerable vocabulary, although the different sounds are all variations on one theme—the familiar, rather raucous bark. Mr. Koch believes that sea-lions also express different meanings (as do the Chinese) by merely changing the pitch of their note" (*ibid.,* p. 49).

The complexity of living forms and functions is something that we are apt to underestimate in speculating on the origins of psychological phenomena. In textbook accounts the facts have to be generalized and simplified to make them comprehensible to beginners; but as soon as you tackle the monographic literature presenting actual cases of growth, maturation, and the conduct of life, and follow actual analyses of function and structure, especially in neurology, the complexity and variability of vital processes are brought home to you with great force. Consider only the chemical activities, that differ enough from any one organism to another to produce the so-called "individuality factor." [9] Or think of the structural organization of the brain; in the small brain center known as the "lateral geniculate body" where the optic nerve ceases to be one bundle of fibers and fans out toward the cortex of the occipital lobe, anatomists have found scores of so-called "boutons," points of reception or emission of electrical impulses, directly on nerve cells, besides the synaptic connections of the branching axons and dendrites of those same cells.[10] The potentialities of such a brain for different courses of activity run into billions and trillions, so that even if inhibiting mechanisms eliminate a hundred thousand connections at a time, the range of possible responses, especially in the crowded circuits of the forebrain, is as good as infinite.

It is very wholesome for a philosopher who tries to

[9] Cf. Leo Loeb, *The Biological Basis of Individuality* (Springfield, Ill., 1945).

[10] Cf. W. H. Marshall and S. A. Talbot, "Recent Evidence for Neural Mechanisms in Vision Leading to a General Theory of Sensory Activity," in H. Klüver, *Visual Mechanisms* (1942), pp. 117–64. "In the cat, optic tract endings in the geniculate divide into several branches and as many as forty ring-shaped boutons have been seen on single radiation cells which may come from as many as ten optic tract fibers. Each fiber also divides to form synapses with several radiation cells. In addition to bouton contacts the radiation cells have numerous dendritic processes, with which the optic tract endings make apparently more numerous synapses . . . than with the radiation cells themselves" (p. 122).
    Cf. R. Lorente de Nó, "Vestibulo-ocular Reflex Arc," *Arch. Neurol. & Psychiat.*, XXX (1933), 245–91. "On each cell in the nervous system numerous synapses, sometimes several thousand, are found. The synapses are always of different kinds, occasionally of ten or more" (p. 279).

conceive of what we call "mind" to take a long look at neurological exhibits, because in psychological studies we usually see and consider only the integrated products —actions and intentions and thoughts—and with regard to speech, words and their uses. Words seem to be the elements of speech; they are the units that keep their essential identity in different relational patterns, and can be separately moved around. They keep their "roots" despite grammatical variations, despite prefixes and suffixes and other modifications. A word is the ultimate semantic element of speech. A large class of our words —most of the nouns, or names—denote objects, and objects are units that can enter into many different situations while keeping their identity, much as words can occur in different statements. This relation gives great support to the conception of words as the units of speech.

And so, I think, they are. But this does not mean that they are original elements of speech, primitive units that were progressively combined into propositions. Communication, among people who inherit language, begins with the word—the baby's or foreigner's unelaborated key word, that stands proxy for a true sentence. But that word has a phylogenetic history, the rise of language, in which probably neither it nor any archaic version of it was an element.

I think it likely that words have actually emerged through progressive simplification of a much more elaborate earlier kind of utterance, which stemmed, in its turn, from several quite diverse sources, and that none of its major sources were forms of animal communication, though some of them were communal.

These are odd-sounding propositions, and I am quite aware of their oddness, but perhaps they are not so fantastic as they sound. They merely depart rather abruptly from our usual background assumptions. For instance, the idea that a relatively simple part of a complex phenomenon might not be one of its primitive factors, but might be a product of progressive simplification, goes against our methodological canons. Ever since Thomas Hobbes set up the so-called genetic method of understanding, we have believed that the simplest concepts into which we could break down our ideas of a complex phenomenon denoted the actual elements of that phenomenon, the factors out of which it was historically compounded. Locke's construction of human experience from pure and simple sense data, Condillac's fancied statue endowed with one form of perception after another, and in our own time Bertrand Russell's "logical atomism," all rest on this belief.[11] But close empirical study of vital processes in nature does not bear it out. A great many advanced behavior patterns *are* elaborations of simpler responses, but some are simplifications of very complicated earlier forms of action. The same holds true of the structures that implement them. When the reflex arc was discovered, physiologists felt themselves in possession of a key to all animal response, for here was a simple unit that could be supposed to engender all higher forms by progressive elaboration. But Herrick and Coghill, through careful studies of salamanders in their larval stages,[12] found that the reflex arc is not a primitive structure ontogenetically at all, but is preceded by much more elaborate arrangements in the embryo that undergo simplifications until a unified afferent-efferent circuit results. This finding was corroborated by Lorente de Nó.[13]

A principle that is operative in the development of an individual is at least possible in the larger development of a stock. There is nothing absurd about the hypothesis that the simple units in a very advanced function, such as human speech, may be simplifications within an earlier more intricate vocal pattern.

Most theories of the origin of language presuppose that man was already man, with social intentions, when he

[11] A belief which has, indeed, been challenged a good many times, but it seems to be ingrained.

[12] C. J. Herrick and G. E. Coghill, "The Development of Reflex Mechanism in Amblystoma," *J. Comp. Neurol.,* XXV (1915).

[13] *Op. cit.,* p. 247. Here the simplification serves for economy; but Gerhardt von Bonin, in his essay, "Types and Similitudes," *Philos. Sc.* XIII (1946), 196–202, observes that "the paleontological evidence has presented cases, such as the ammonites, where evolution produced at first more and more complicated, and later simpler and simpler forms" (p. 198).

began to speak.[14] But in fact, man must have been an animal—a high primate, with a tendency to live in droves like most of the great apes—when he began to speak. And it must have been rather different from the ancient progenitors of our apes, which evidently lacked, or at least never possessed in combination, those traits that have eventuated in speech.

What were those traits? Speech is such a complex function that it has probably not arisen from any single source. Yet if it developed naturally in the hominid stock, every one of its constituents must have started from some spontaneous animal activity, not been invented for a purpose; for only human beings invent instruments for a purpose preconceived. Before speech there is no conception; there are only perceptions, and a characteristic repertoire of actions, and a readiness to act according to the enticements of the perceived world. In speech as we know it, however, there seems to be one flowing, articulate symbolic act in which conventional signs are strung together in conventional ways without much trouble, and similar processes evoked in other persons, all as nicely timed as a rally of ping-pong. Nothing seems more integral and self-contained than the outpouring of language in conversation. How is one ever to break it down into primitive acts?

It was from the psychiatric literature on language—on aphasia, paraphasia, agrammatism, alexia, and kindred subjects—that something like a guiding principle emerged. The most baffling thing about the cerebral disturbances of speech is, what strange losses people can sustain: loss of grammatical form without any loss or confusion of words, so that the patient can speak only in "telegraph style"; or contrariwise, loss or confusion of words without loss of sentence structure, so that speech flows in easy sentencelike utterances, but only the prepositions, connectives, and vocal punctuations are

14 E.g., Lord Haldane, *op. cit.*, says, "A *Pithecanthropus* child which gave the danger call or the food discovery call without due cause was probably punished" (p. 398). But animals do not punish their young for mischief done; the "cuffing" a cub may receive from its mother is always interference with its momentary annoying act, to stop it. The concept of a *deed*, and hence praise and punishment, belong to human life.

recognizable; the informative words all garbled or sense-less.[15] Lewis Carroll's

> 'T was brillig, and the slithy toves
> Did gyre and gimble in the wabe

illustrates this separation of sentence form and verbal content. There may be inability to understand spoken language, but not inability to understand printed or written language,[16] yet without any defect of hearing, or the other way about—inability to read, but not to understand speech—without any ocular trouble.[17] There are cases of alexia for words but not for letters,[18] and the recognition, naming, and using of numbers are often intact where neither letters nor words can be recognized.[19] Furthermore, some brain injuries leave the victim able to repeat words spoken for him, but not to speak spontaneously, and others make him unable to repeat words just heard, but not unable to utter them in spontaneous speech. There are even several cases on record of persons in whom a cerebral lesion caused inability to name any inanimate object, but not inability to name living things, or call people by their proper names, and, conversely, cases of inability to name persons, animals, or any parts of them, but not to find the words for inanimate objects like watches and slippers.[20]

In the face of these peculiar, sometimes really bizarre exhibits, it occurred to me that what can be separately lost from the integral phenomenon of speech may have

15 See esp. M. Isserlin, "Ueber Agrammatismus," *Ztschr. f. ges. Neurol. u. Psychiat.,* LXXV (1922), 332–410.

16 H. Kogerer, "Worttaubheit, Melodientaubheit, Gebärdeagnosie," *Ztschr. f. ges. Neurol. u. Psychiat.,* XCII (1924), 469–83; see also H. Liepmann and M. Pappenheim, "Ueber einen Fall von sogenannter Leitungsaphasie mit anatomischen Befund," *Ztschr. f. ges. Neurol. u. Psychiat.,* XXVII (1915), 1–41.

17 All these special forms are listed in J. M. Nielsen's *Agnosia, Apraxia, Aphasia* (New York, 1946).

18 Goodhart and Savitsky, "Alexia Following Injuries of the Head," *Arch. Neurol. & Psychiat.,* XXX (1933), 223–24.

19 F. Grewel, "Acalculia," *Brain,* LXXV (1952), 397–407.

20 J. M. Nielsen, "Visual Agnosia for Animate Objects: Report of a Case with Autopsy," *Tr. Am. Neurol. Assn.* (1942), 128–30.

been separately developed in the prehistoric, prehuman brain. Here is at least a working notion of a new way to break down the verbal process that might yield a new conception of what has gone into it.

In singling out such elements, and trying to trace them back to some plausible—though of course hypothetical —prehuman proclivities, one meets with the surprising fact that some of these habits, that may be supposed to have prepared speech, actually exist in the animal kingdom, and are even quite highly developed, sometimes in relatively low animals. But they are far from any kind of speech. They are raw, unassembled materials, that would be needed in conjunction, as a foundation, if speech were to arise. In the prehuman primate they must have coincided at some time to provide that foundation.

This principle of analysis takes us much further back into preparatory phases of mental development than the usual anthropological approach to the problem of speech, which reaches back only to the supposed archaic forms of genuine language. Not only mental activities, but some grosser somatic conditions that made them possible, must have met in the animal stock that produced the human race. For instance, the continuity of language requires a bodily mechanism that can sustain a long process of vocalization. Not all animals can do that; it is interesting that the chimpanzee, which is nearest to man in mental capacity, cannot sustain a vowel sound; also it rarely produces a pure and simple sound. Its larynx is too complicated, and it has more than one source of air supply for it, and no fine control of a single set of bellows to mete out its vocal power.[21] The gibbon has a simpler larynx, more like ours, and also the requisite propensity to utter long, chantlike ululations in chorus: that is, it has the physical powers of vocalization, and the habit of using them in a gathered company—two prerequisites for speech.[22] But its brain is too inferior to endow its joyful noise with anything but self-expression and mutual stimulation to keep it up.

21 See G. Kelemen, "Structure and Performance in Animal Language," *Arch. Otolaryngol.*, L (1949), 740–44.

22 L. Boutan, *op. cit.*, esp. pp. 30–31.

Another condition of speech is the epicritical ear, that distinguishes one sound from another, beyond the usual distinction of noises according to their sources—that is, beyond distinguishing them as calls of other creatures, as footsteps, perhaps as the splash of water, and for the rest either as meaningless rumbles and creaks, or not at all. The epicritical power of hearing requires a highly specialized cochlea and a distribution of the auditory nerve in the brain that is not found in all the higher animals, but occurs in several birds—an anomalous development in a relatively low type of brain. Those birds that imitate the whistles of other birds and the sounds of human speech, whereby we know they have a highly analytic hearing (which anatomical findings bear out), [23] have something more that is relevant to our own powers: the control of the vocal apparatus by the ear, which seems to be rudimentary in most animals, although the mechanisms of hearing and sound-making are always associated—even in the cricket, which has its peripheral organs of hearing in the thighs.[24] The kind of feedback that molds an utterance according to sounds heard, and makes formal imitation possible, is another specialization beyond the epicritical receptor organ. Dogs have the fine receptor, the ear that discriminates articulate sounds within a general category, for they can respond selectively to quite a gamut of verbal signals, and Pavlov found their discrimination of tonal pitch superior to man's; but dogs never show the slightest impulse or ability to imitate foreign sounds.

So we find several prerequisites for speech—sustained and variable vocalization, the tendency to responsive utterance, the epicritical hearing and fine control of vocalization by the ear that implement imitation—prefigured in the behavior patterns of widely different animals. Yet none of those animals use language. These

[23] Otto Kalischer, "Das Grosshirn der Papageien in anatomischer und physiologischer Beziehung," *Abhandl. königl.-Preuss. Akad. Wissensch.*, IV (1905), 1–105; a study based on ten years' work of training, operating, retraining, and finally autopsying some sixty talking parrots.

[24] Louis Guggenheim, *Phylogenesis of the Ear* (Culver City, Calif., 1948), p. 78.

traits are only some of its conditions, and even they do not coincide in any one species. In the protohuman primate they must have coincided—not only with each other, but with some further ones as well, that may or may not occur in other creatures.

The decisive function in the making of language comes, I think, from quite another quarter than the vocal-auditory complexes that serve its normal expression. That other quarter is the visual system, in which the visual image—the paradigm of what, therefore, we call "imagination"—almost certainly is produced.

How a visual image is engendered and what nervous mechanisms participate in its creation no one has yet described; I have gathered a few ideas on the subject, but they need not detain us here. The important thing is that images are the things that naturally take on the character of symbols. Images are "such stuff as dreams are made on"; dreams have the tendency to assume symbolic value, apparently very early in our lives, and the peculiar involutions of meaning in their imagery, the vagueness of connections, the spontaneity of their presentations, and the emotional excitement of any very vivid dream may well reflect the nature of primitive symbolic experience.

The old problem, how words became attached to objects as their distinctive names, and how they became generalized so that they denoted kinds of things rather than individuals, may find its solution if we can give up the notion that primitive man *invented* speech, and agreed on names for things and other basic conventions. I do not believe names were originally assigned to things at all; *naming* is a process that presupposes speech. Now that we have language, we can give names to new comets, new gadgets, and constantly to new babies. But in the making of speech, I think it more likely that definite phonetic structures were already at hand, developed in another context, and that meanings accrued to them—vaguely and variably at first, but by natural processes that tended to specify and fix them. Such meanings were not pragmatic signal values of specific sounds for specific things; several eminent psychiatrists to the contrary not-

withstanding,[25] primitive denotation was not like using
a proper name. When words took shape, they were general in intent, from the beginning; their connotations in-
hered in them, and their denotations were whatever fitted
this inherent sense.

Now that I have thus pontificated on what happened,
let me explain why I think something like this must have
happened, and how it would account for the greatest of
all mysteries of language—the fact that language is symbolic, when no animal utterance shows any tendency that
way. The biological factors that caused this great shift
in the vocal function were, I believe, the development of
visual imagery in the humanoid brain, and the part it
came to play in a highly exciting, elating experience, the
festal dance. (How prehuman beings advanced from animal behavior to formalized tribal dance is another relevant subject I cannot broach here.) The mental image
was, I think, the catalyst that precipitated the conceptual
import of speech.

As I remarked before, images are more prone than
anything else we know to become symbols; they have
several attributes that work together to make them symbolic. So it was another of the evolutionary coincidences
that the Calibans who preceded us suffered a peculiar
specialization in their visual systems, so that we produce
mental images without even trying—most successfully, in
fact, while we sleep.

There is a reason, of course, why this should be a
hominid specialty, and we can at least guess what caused

25 Sylvano Arieti, "The Possibility of Psychosomatic Involvement of the Central Nervous System in Schizophrenia," *J. Nervous & Mental Disease,* CXXIII (1956), 324–33, esp. 332; where
he (with whose views of symbol formation I agree in some respects, as will shortly be apparent), for instance, holds that in a
primordial family a baby might babble "ma-ma" and associate
the utterance "with the mother or with the image of the mother," and that "if a second sibling understands that the sound ma-
ma refers to mother, language is originated. . . . But at this level
the sound ma-ma denotes, but does not possess much connotation
power."

See also J. S. Kasanin, "The Disturbance of Conceptual Thinking in Schizophrenia," in *Language and Thought in Schizophrenia,*
ed. by J. S. Kasanin and N. D. C. Lewis (Berkeley, Calif., 1944):
". . . when the child says 'table' or 'chair' he does not mean tables
or chairs in general, but the table or chair which is in his house
or which belongs to him."

our odd and rather impractical habit of *visualizing,* with and without stimulation from the end organs, the eyes. The human brain presumably developed, like any animal brain we know, as a mediating organ between afferent impulses and their efferent completion, that is, their spending themselves in action. In animals, typically, every stimulation that takes effect at all is spent in some overt act, which may be anything from a reflex twitch of the skin to a directed act of the whole aroused creature. But the messages which come into our brains are so many and various that it would be impossible and exhausting to spend each afferent impulse in overt action. So a great many, especially the countless visual impressions we take in, have to be finished within the brain; the cerebral response is the formation of an image. This automatic process may occur in animals, too, but sporadically and at a lower intensity, and therefore without further consequences. If animals have images, I don't think they are bothered by them or use them; such passing visions may be like our after-images, automatic products of sensory stimulation.[26]

In human beings, however, image making has become a normal conclusion for acts of focused gazing. Since, in the waking state, it is easier to look at things than not to, image production is generally effortless and unintentional, and in the normal course of development soon becomes so rich that there is a constant play of imagery. Every impression is apt to produce an image, however briefly and incompletely, and out of this welter a few more definite visualizations emerge at intervals.

The several characteristics that make the mental image prone to become symbolic are, in the first place, this spontaneous, quasi-automatic production; secondly, a tendency of image-making processes to mesh, and pool their results; then, their origin in actual perception which gives images an obvious relation to the sources of perception—things perceived—a relation we call "represen-

26 This difference in the frequency, intensity, and clarity of images, in human and animal brains, is strikingly corroborated and anatomically explained by Niess von Mayendorf, "Ueber den vasomotorischen Mechanismus der Halluzinationen," *Ztschr. f. ges. Neurol. u. Psychiat.,* CXIV (1928), 311–22.

tation"; furthermore, the very important fact that an image, once formed, can be reactivated in many ways, by all sorts of external and internal stimulations; and finally, its involvement with emotion. Let us consider what each of these traits has to do with the making of the primitive symbol, and with the enlistment of the vocal organs for its projection.

A biological mechanism that is about to assume a new function is usually developed at least somewhat beyond the needs of its original function—that is, its activity has a certain amount of play, sometimes called "excess energy," which allows unpredictable developments. A new departure is not likely to be based on rare occurrences, for to become established it has to survive many miscarriages, and that means that it has to begin over and over again—that is, the conditions for it have to be generous. So, in a brain where imagination was to take on a new and momentous function—symbolization—the production of images had to be a vigorous business, generating images all the time, so that most of them could be wasted, and the symbolic activity could still begin again and again, and proceed to various degrees, without interfering with the normal functions of the brain in the whole organic economy. So the normality and ease of image producing met one of the first requisites for the rise of a higher function.[27]

The second important feature of mental images for symbol making is the fact that the processes of imagination seem particularly prone to affect each other, to mingle and mesh and share their paths of activity, inhibiting or reinforcing nervous impulses in progress, and especially inducing all sorts of neighboring reactions. Consequently their products tend to fuse: images that share some features fuse into one image with emphasis on those features, which thereby are stressed, and dominate the

---

[27] This fact is mentioned by P. L. Short in his paper, "The Objective Study of Mental Imagery," *Brit. J. Psychol.*, XLIV (1953), 38–51, where he writes: ". . . in thinking, it is the images that occur most readily and habitually that are important, not the ones thought to be most 'intense' or 'vivid' at a given moment. The mere emergence of very vivid images may not be associated at all with the tendency to have and to use images" (p. 38). He also notes the importance of the connection between percepts and centrally produced images.

welter of other characters that, for their part, are weakened by fusion. Images, therefore, modify each other; some dominate others, and all tend to become simplified. Emphasis is what gives contours and gradients and other structural elements to images. Emphasis is the natural process of abstraction, whereby our visual representations are made to differ from the direct perceptions that started them. Rudolph Arnheim in his book, *Art and Visual Perception,*[28] has gone quite deeply into the distinctions between the laws of perception and those of representation. The point of interest here is that the power of abstract symbolic thinking, which plays such a great part in later human mentality, rests on a relatively primitive talent of abstractive seeing that comes with the nature of the visual image.[29]

The third major condition is simply the fact that images stem from percepts, and the process of their derivation is an original continuity of a peripheral event, the effect of a visible object on the eye, with the further nervous events that terminate in the formation of an image in the brain. The eye is the end organ of the visual apparatus; what goes on behind the retina, and especially, perhaps, beyond the chiasma, is the rest of our seeing, with all its reverberations and complications and their astounding effects. The recognition of an image as something connected with the external world is intuitive,[30] as the response to external things in direct visual perception, which all seeing animals exhibit, is instinctive. This recognition of images as representations of visible

[28] Berkeley, Calif., 1954.

[29] Some interesting comments on abstractive seeing may also be found in Leo Steinberg's paper, "The Eye is a Part of the Mind," *Partisan Rev.,* XX (1953), 194–212; reprinted in *Reflections on Art* (Baltimore, 1958). There are also various studies of the neural processes involved in such sensory abstraction, e.g., D. M. Purdy, "The Structure of the Visual World," *Psychol. Rev.,* XLIII (1936), 59–82, esp. Pt. III; Fred Attneave's technological essay, "Some Informational Aspects of Visual Perception," *Psychol. Rev.,* LXI (1954), 183–93; Norbert Wiener's *Cybernetics* (New York, 1948); and especially in a study by W. H. Marshall and S. A. Talbot, "Recent Evidence for Neural Mechanisms in Vision Leading to a General Theory of Sensory Acuity," in H. Klüver, *Visual Mechanisms* (1942), pp. 117–64.

[30] Cf. D. Forsyth, "The Infantile Psyche, with Special Reference to Visual Projection," *Brit. J. Psychol.,* XI (1920/1), 263–76.

things is the basis on which the whole public importance of symbols is built—their use for reference. But there must have been another coincidence to make that happen.

This crucial fourth factor is really part of that lability of imagination, and openness to influence, that we have already remarked; but more precisely, it is the fact that the occurrence of an image may be induced by a great many different kinds of stimulation, either from outside the organism or from within.[31] Often one cannot tell what evokes a mental image; sometimes a whole situation that often recurs will always do it; for instance, whenever you step out on a pier and smell salt water you may have an image of your first sailboat. Even the salt smell alone may invoke it. So may the mention of the boat's name. Those are more specific stimuli, but there can be all kinds. This readiness to occur in a total context, but also to be touched off by small fragments of that context encountered in other settings, is the trait that frees the mental image from its original connection with peripheral vision, that is, from the thing it first represented. Add to this the tendency of images with traits in common to fuse and make a simplified image —that is, to become schematic—and you see how much of our image making would become casual acts of ideation, without any specific memory bonds to perceptual experiences. Not only the images themselves that share a schematic character, but also their representational functions fuse; any one of them can represent the original percept of any other; that is, as representations whole families of them can stand proxy one for another. Any image of a grasshopper can represent any grasshopper we have actually seen that was not so distinctive that it created an image too different to fit the schema. If such an oddity appears we form an image of a *special kind* of grasshopper. With its liberation from perception the image becomes general; and as soon as it can represent

31 D. Forsyth, *op. cit.*, p. 265: "The visual organ . . . transmits a centripetal wave of excitement which is registered in the mind as a memorative impression of the excitation. This visual memory becomes associated with inner (somatic) excitations, and can subsequently be activated from either of the two directions in which it has established excitatory connections."

something else than its own original stimulus, it becomes a symbol. Schematic similarities in otherwise distinct images make it possible to recall one object through the image of another. Thus, for instance, the outline of the new moon is like that of a small curved boat. We can see the moon as a canoe, or a canoe as a moon. Either assimilation reinforces the perception of shape. This is the natural process of abstraction. We speak of the sickle, the bowl, the disk of the moon in its various phases. In developed thinking we know whether we are talking about the moon or about a boat—that is, we know which image is standing proxy for the other. But studies in the symbolic functions occurring in dream and myth and some psychoses give support to the belief that this is a sober insight which was probably not very early.[32] At the level of prehuman image mongering, the question is rather how one image, even without sensory support, becomes dominant over others, so that they are its symbolic representatives in imagination.

Here, the mechanism seems to be the connection of imagery with emotion. In the complex of images, the one most charged with emotion becomes the dominant image which all the others repeat, reinforce, and represent within the brain itself, even below the level of awareness —in the limbo of what Freud called "the dream work," whereby the significant images, the symbols for conception, are made.

These are, I think, the main physical and behavioral factors that must have existed conjointly in the one ani-

---

[32] The sources substantiating this proposition are too scattered and numerous to quote. One of the first explicit statements of it is found in an article which has become a classic—Herbert Silberer's "Ueber die Symbolbildung," *Jahrb. f. psychoanalyt. u. Psychopathol. Forsch.*, III (1912), 661–723, republished in English translation, unfortunately with some deletions, in David Rapaport's anthology, *Organization and Pathology of Thought* (New York, 1951). Silberer wrote: "A people which speaks in metaphors does not experience what it says as metaphoric; the symbols it uses are regarded by it not as symbols, but rather as realities . . ." (Rapaport, p. 212). They certainly all contradict the claim of Jean-Paul Sartre in *L' Imagination* (Paris, 1948), p. 104, that one never mistakes a fantasy image for a percept: "Aucune image, jamais, ne vient se mêler aux choses réelles" (p. 109). And further: ". . . il m' est impossible de former une image sans savoir en même temps que je forme une image . . ." (p. 110).

mal species that has developed speech: the power of elaborate vocalization, the discriminative ear that heard patterns of sounds, the nervous mechanisms that controlled utterance by hearing inner and outer sounds, and the tendency to utter long passages of sound in gatherings of many individuals—that is, the habit of joint ululation —with considerable articulation that recurred at about the same point within every such occasion, and, in these same beings, the high mental activity that issued in visual image making. The gatherings were probably communal rituals, or rather, awesome aesthetic precursors of genuine ritual, the ululations the vocal elements in primitive dance. This idea was propounded long ago by J. Donovan,[33] but no one seems to have paid much attention to it. I adopted it in an early book, *Philosophy in a New Key*, and the more I reflect on it the more I think it is sound. It was Donovan's idea that words were not primitive elements in human utterance when it became symbolic, but that meaning first accrued to longer passages, which were gradually broken or condensed into separate bits, each with its own fixed sense. But what he did not say—and I did not see, twenty years ago— was how conceptual meaning accrued to any vocal products at all. I certainly never realized what part the private mental image played in preparing the way for symbolic language—that the whole mechanism of symbolization was probably worked out in the visual system before its power could be transferred to the vocal-auditory realm. Now, with that helpful surmise, let us see how the transfer would be possible, and not too improbable.

In the elaborate development of tribal dance all individuals of the primitive horde became familiar with the vocal sounds that belonged to various sequences of steps and gestures, some perhaps mimetic, others simply athletic, but working up to climaxes of excitement. The "song," or vocal part of the dance, became more and more differentiated with the evolution of the gestic patterns. At high points there were undoubtedly special

33 "The Festal Origin of Human Speech," *Mind,* XVI, o.s. (1891), 498–506, and XVII (1892), 325–39.

shouts and elaborate halloos. In the overstimulated brains of the celebrants, images must have been evoked at these points of action and special vocalization—images that tended to recur in that context, until for each individual his own symbolic images were built into the familiar patterns of tribal rituals. A dance passage takes time and energy and usually several persons to produce, but the vocal ingredient can be produced with little effort and a minimum of time by any individual. To remember the dance would bring the vocal element to his throat; as the memory of playing "London Bridge" will usually cause a child to hum the tune,

"Lon-don Bridge is fal-ling down,"

with no thought of a bridge or a fair lady, but of the game. So people could reactivate their emotional symbolic images by a snatch of the festal songs. If the dance action is, say, swinging a club, or even feels like that familiar and expansive act, the various images evoked will be of a club, or clubs, or raising or swinging clubs, or cracking them against each other. It is the image that symbolizes the activity and the objects involved in it. The image is the magical effect of the sound pattern when it is intoned apart from the dance.

The image is a pure conception; it does not signalize or demand its object, but denotes it. Of course, this denotative symbol, the image, begets no communication, for it is purely private. But the things imaged are public, and the sounds that activate images are public; they affect everybody by evoking images at roughly the same moments of dance action. Within a fairly wide range it does not matter how different the private images are. They are equivalent symbols for the act or the objects that mark those stations in the ritual where the vocal bits belong, which may be uttered out of context by some individual; and suddenly meaning accrues to the phrase, other beings *understand,* especially if a connoted object is physically at hand, apart from its ritual context.

I suspect that the first meanings of such secularized vocalization were very vague; swing a club, hit a man with a club, kill man and beast, whirl and hit, get hit, wave a club at the moon—may all have belonged by

turns to one long utterance, in which the separate articulate parts need not have had any separable meanings.[34]
But once such passages were used to evoke ideas, their
vocalization would quickly become modified, especially
by reduction to the *speaking voice,* which can utter its
sounds with more speed and less effort than any singing
voice. This everyday utterance would tend to emphasize
vowels and consonants—that is, mouth articulations—to
replace distinctions of pitch. Some languages today use
tonal distinctions, without precise pitch, as semantic devices. But in most human speech, tones serve only for
punctuation and emotional coloring.

The great step from anthropoid to anthropos, animal
to man, was taken when the vocal organs were moved to
register the occurrence of an image, and stirred an equivalent occurrence in another brain, and the two creatures
referred to the same thing. At that point, the vocal habit
that had long served for communion assumed the function of communication. To evoke ideas in each other's
minds, not in the course of action, but of emotion and
memory—that is, in reflection—is to communicate *about*
something, and that is what no animals do.

From then on, speech probably advanced with headlong speed; the vaguely articulated phrases of the gathered horde contracted around their cores of meaning
and made long, rich, omnibus words, and broke up into
more specifically denotative words, until practically the
whole phonetic repertoire was formalized into separable
bits, and language entered the synthetic stage of making
sentences out of words—the reverse of its pristine ar-
ticulative process. The new motive of communication
must have driven it like wildfire. At this stage if not
before, the actual evocation of images became dispensa-
ble. We do not need vision to learn speech. The symbolic function has passed to the act of speech itself,
and from there finally to the word itself, so that even
hearing may be prosthetically replaced. For when ver-
balization is complete, people have not only speech, but
language.

---

[34] In the *Encyclopaedia Britannica* (1957 ed., *s.v.* "Language"),
Otto Jespersen voices the same opinion.

I think there were other uses of speechlike utterance, too—the principle of tracking down the elements of language that may be separately lost by cerebral impairment even today leads in many directions. Proper names may not have had the same origin as genuine nouns, and numerals are something different again; onomatopoetic words, too, seem to have had their own genesis, apart from the main source of language. But under the influence of language all utterances tended to become words. This is still the case. For instance, our expletives, that have no real verbal meaning in present-day language, always fall under its influence. Only a German says "ach"—most Americans cannot even pronounce it—he says "au" where an American says "ouch;" and who but a Frenchwoman would ever say "ou-la-la"?

Once communication got started, the rise of human mentality may have been cataclysmic, a matter of a few generations wherever it began at all. It must have been an exciting and disconcerting phase of our history. We have traces of it even to this day in the holy fear in which many people hold divine names, blessings, curses, magic formulas—all verbal fragments, imbued with the mystic power of thought that came with speech.

In looking back over all these processes that must have come together to beget language, I am struck by a few outstanding facts: in the first place, the depth to which the foundations go, on which this highest of all creature attainments is built; secondly, the complexity of all living functions, for every one of those preparatory traits was itself a highly integrated complex of many nervous processes; in the third place, the fact that not one of the constituents in the new and fateful talent was a mode of animal communication. It seems most likely that the office of communication was taken over by speech, from entirely different activities, when speech was well started; but undoubtedly communication was what henceforth made its history. Finally, it is a notable fact that the two senses which hold the greatest places in the human cortex, sight and hearing, were both needed to produce language; neither a sightless nor a deaf race could have evolved it. If man could either hear no evil or see no evil, he could speak no evil—nor yet any good.

3 ON A NEW DEFINITION OF "SYMBOL"*

IN EVERY AGE, philosophical thinking exploits some dominant concepts and makes its greatest headway in solving problems conceived in terms of them. The seventeenth- and eighteenth-century philosophers construed knowledge, knower, and known in terms of sense data and their association. Descartes's self-examination gave classical psychology *the mind and its contents* as a starting point. Locke set up sensory immediacy as the new criterion of the real, namely, the "really given"— James's and Whitehead's "stubborn, ineluctable fact." Hobbes provided the *genetic method* of building up complex ideas from simple ones, as one builds a wall of bricks or a puzzle picture from many pieces. So Berkeley and Hume built tables out of squareness and brownness (Russell took a final fling at this job by using "soft data" as his logical glue); and in another quarter, still true to the Hobbesian method, Pavlov built intellect out of conditioned reflexes and Loeb built life out of tropisms.

The next century, opening with the accomplished work of Kant, had a new dominant notion, the transcendental sources of experience. This begot the problems of subject and object, concept and percept, and worst of all, form and content. Empiricism and transcendentalism went their respective ways, one panting after the headlong advance of science, the other sidling toward religion; and each repudiated the very issues that seemed obvious and pressing to the other.

We inherit both lines of thought. Forty years ago

* This paper was presented at Brown University in 1956.

this legacy seemed enough to make philosophers schizophrenic. But since then a strange development (which had already started even at the worst time of schism, the turn of the century) has become apparent: empiricism as well as transcendentalism uncovered a new level of philosophical problems, below the superficial divergent "isms." Both struck the rich vein of *semantic* issues.

The concept of meaning, in all its varieties, is the dominant philosophical concept of our time. Sign, symbol, denotation, signification, communication—these notions are our stock in trade. The changing frame of scientific thought inspired the semantic shift from attributive to operational definition. The bold expansion of mathematics broached some tricky problems of incomplete symbols, purely structural signs, variable context, variable sense, indirect reference; modern symbolic logic has advanced chiefly under the goad of such puzzling ideas. It has become the basic technique of the most modern philosophical thinking, and a technique is a natural measure of a so-called "field of study." To lend meaning to mathematics has been the first aim of our semantic labors, and the concepts developed in symbolic logic—concepts like "element," "relation," "proposition," "class," and the directive notions of "assertion," "definition," "substitution," and so on—have served to organize the new realm. But mathematics has not remained the only challenger; an even greater task has arisen for the philosopher with the growth of the physical sciences, whereof mathematics is the handmaid (a highly modern, independent maid—rather an Amazon). It is with regard to the sciences of nature that all the problems of *reference* arise; and these 'in turn entail epistemological questions of truth, fact, knowledge, and —coming full circle back to semantics—communication of knowledge.

Every new venture in philosophy has a furiously active phase, reaches a crest of important production, and then slows to a more sober sort of work as its inherent paradoxes, its difficulties of conception, come to light. Then it either elicits a real growth of people's intellectual faculties, an advance of imagination, like the shift from substance-attribute thinking to functional thinking that marks scientific imagination today, and enlarges its field by bold extensions of its generative concepts, or it bogs down on its paradoxes, as even very ardent philosophical speculations—notoriously social and ethical ones—have often done.

Semantic theory has, I think, already passed its first crest. Its paradoxes have appeared, and the desire to evade them tends to narrow the field of inquiry to a few carefully put subjects. If you run back the table of contents of a journal like *Mind* from the current number to the 1920's, there is no great change in the titles. John Wisdom on "denoting" might be 1928, 1938, or 1948. The new contributors of the Cambridge school are fending off rather than attacking semantic problems —rolling them all up again in the careless colloquial language of common sense, from which they were originally extricated. That is one way of dealing with paradoxes.

The whole study of symbols and meaning seems to me to be temporarily exhausted, and bogging down. At the same time, an outside danger besets what conquests have been made, for the interest in symbols is not limited to the critique of science and interpretation of mathematics, but is stirring in fairly remote quarters— psychology (after two kinds), ethnology, and philology. In some of these contexts the very conception of "symbol" is different from that used by a mathematician or scientist. A symbol may be a myth, a root metaphor, or a clinical symptom. "Meaning," likewise, is neither signification nor denotation. It is anything from a stimulus-response relation, to the wish behind a dream.

There is little the poor epistemologist can do about such encroachments of the jungle on his garden. All he can say is that these are loose and illicit uses of the words "symbol" and "meaning." Yet the uses go on, and even develop techniques, in which it is hard to see a mere loose treatment of ideas once belonging to logic. The symbol concept of dynamic psychology, for instance, is obviously of different origin from that employed by Whitehead and Russell in *Principia mathematica*. The fact is that several major lines of thought have arrived almost simultaneously at the recognition of the basic mental function that distinguishes man from nonhuman creatures—the use, in one way or another, of symbols to convey concepts.

It must be admitted that one way is very different from another. Now, any phenomenon that can serve in such diverse ways must be fairly complex. It is likely to have many interrelated functions. In any given context, some of its functions are likely to be more important or more obvious than others, and the concept of the phenomenon itself (here, the concept of "symbol") will be defined with reference to its relevant properties. The definition establishes but also restricts it; and it may happen that the most adequate and economical definition we can make in a fairly precise context, such as the context of logical discourse in which "symbol" has been defined, is incapable of yielding any derivative concepts that might serve other interests. It allows of no generalization, no *wider sense*. Therefore it cannot be extended to any very different frames of reference.

It was in reflecting on the nature of art that I came on a conception of the symbol relation quite distinct from the one I had formed in connection with all my earlier studies, which had centered around symbolic logic. This new view of symbolization and meaning stemmed from the Kantian analysis of experience, and had been highly developed in Cassirer's *Philosophie der symbolischen Formen*. In many years of work on the fundamental problems of art I have found it indispensable; it served as a key to the most involved questions. But this symbol concept, as it emerges in use, in the course of work—which, after all, is the most authentic source of all concepts—cannot be defined in terms of denotation, signification, formal assignment, or reference. The proof of a pudding is in the eating, and I submit that Cassirer's pudding is good; but the recipe is not on the box. Cassirer himself considered the semantic functions that belong to scientific symbols as a special development, which occurred under the influence of language, by virtue of its inherent *generality* together with its *signific* character. But symbolization as such he traced further back. His notion of "symbol" was more primitive than that of a sign used by common consent to stand for an associated concept; in his sense of the word, a sound, mark, object, or event could be a symbol to a person, without that person's consciously going from it to its meaning. This is the basic concept in his theory of myth.

A similar idea meets us in Freud's theory of dreams. Cassirer opposed that theory vehemently. It was, however, not Freud's symbol concept he rejected, but the subjective nature of the meaning Freud attributed to it. We need not go into this question; what is relevant here is merely that two thinkers with different interests and aims have worked extensively and effectively with a concept that logicians and philosophers of science find unintelligible.

The fact that three large subjects—myth, art, and dynamic psychology—are made accessible to progressive study by the use of a wide, but logically questionable conception of "symbol," and consequently of "meaning," "knowledge," and other *definienda* connected with "symbol," makes me suspect that the terms in which our semantic definitions are traditionally couched militate against their generalization, and thereby against legitimate extensions of our metalogical concepts. If the formally defined sense of "symbol" and the problematical sense derived from new uses cannot be commensurated, they will simply diverge until the word has two unrelated meanings—not a desirable prospect, in an age that dreams of the unity of science. Above all, such a practice would court the danger that where the word "symbol" is simply left undefined, it will increase without limit in vagueness, and collect the aura of emotional values that usually accrues to illicitly extended terms. My recommendation, therefore, is to try a new definition altogether, that may lend itself to wider uses, but allow the closest specification in formal contexts.

Most semanticists have approached the study of symbols with a primary interest in discursive thought and its communication, i.e., their obvious functions in discourse. During recent years the emphasis has shifted more and more toward communication. There are some interesting reasons for this tendency, but they do not concern us here. What concerns us is the stress which has thereby been laid on two properties of symbols that are usually taken as essential characteristics: the function of *reference,* or direction of the user's interest to something apart from the symbol, and the *conventional* nature of the connection between the symbol and the object to which it refers, by virtue of which connection the reference occurs. Ernest Nagel has defined the scientist's concept of "symbol" in the statement: "By a symbol I understand any occurrence (or type of occurrence), usually linguistic in status, which is taken to signify something else by way of tacit or explicit conventions or rules of language." [1]

This is, I think, a sufficient characterization of "symbol" for all purposes of science, and indeed all literal uses of language, including idiomatic and colloquially figurative uses. The rules of using language need not be strict to be publicly though tacitly accepted conventions. In most cases of figurative statement, the literal equivalent is directly understood, and could be readily produced by the speaker or writer using the figure of speech, which is itself a further convention.

Nagel is quite aware of the fact that the word "symbol" has some uses to which this definition would not be adequate, and takes care to point it out. In the essay from which I just quoted, he does not censure those other uses as illicit, though he has questioned their credentials elsewhere. But the thing that concerns me here is precisely the ground on which he could and did question them—namely, that a symbol concept appropriate to those other uses cannot be derived by any modification of the scientific concept. No generalization of the definition he has given, followed by a different specification, will yield a meaning of "symbol" usable in the contexts where obviously a different meaning obtains.

Our interest in communication had led us to note, above all, those kinds of symbol that lend themselves to this purpose; some semantic theories, especially the classic doctrines that go back to the eighteenth century,

[1] "Symbolism and Science," in *Symbols and Values: An Initial Study* (Thirteenth Symposium on Science, Philosophy and Religion; New York, 1954).

treat communication as the original function of language, and indeed of all symbolization. Modern psychological studies of language often present symbols as glorified signals (what Nagel distinguishes as "natural signs"), in the hope of finding their prototypes in animal communication. The importance of language as a human communicative device is certainly patent.

But this paramount use has made us neglect another aspect of symbols, which is less obvious, but perhaps, at some levels of our mental evolution, equally important—the *formulation* of experience by the process of symbolization. This aspect has not gone entirely unrecognized. It is the great insight of those epistemological thinkers who take their inspiration from Kant. Kant, of course, realized and declared that the human mind puts its stamp on experience, that it receives no raw data for its perceptions, but that everything humanly perceivable is already held in the mold of the humanly conceivable. The innate schema, however, is transcendental, common to all human consciousness; it furnishes no principle of conceptual advance, no phenomenal means of conception. Its imposition is not a phenomenal process. Yet the formulation of experience is a phenomenal process. Again it was, above all, Cassirer who recognized the part which *symbolization,* or symbolic expression, plays in the formulation of things and events and the natural ordering of our ambient as a "world."

This formulative function is common to all symbols, though in some it is very elementary. Any sign—for instance, the little noise that a word physically is—by being conventionally *assigned* to any object, event, quality, relation, or what not that it is to signify, bestows a conceptual identity on that designated item. Symbolization gives it form.

The perception of form arises, I think, from the process of symbolization, and the perception of form is abstraction. Abstraction is usually treated as a difficult, unnatural process—Bergson would have us believe, indeed, that it is an antinatural process of perceptual distortion. But from the naturalistic view which, for better or worse, I find compelling, it is hard to understand how anyone could have started any abstractive practices if abstraction were not natural to human minds.[2] The fact is, I think, that the perception of forms, or abstraction, is intuitive, just as the recognition of relations, of instances, and of meaning is. It is one of the basic acts of logical intuition, and its primitive and typical occurrence is in the process of symbolization.

I should like to propose a definition of "symbol" based on this formulative function, by means of which some sort of *conception* is always abstracted from any symbolized experience. In a book published only three years ago, I defined a symbol as "any device whereby we are enabled to make an abstraction." I am already doubtful of that definition in its simple, initial form, though it may prove to be tenable. On the other hand, it may be that some devices whereby we make an abstraction are not complete, bona fide symbols, but that it is safer—at least tentatively—to say: "Any device whereby we make an abstraction is a symbolic element, and all abstraction involves symbolization." Whatever the precise wording should finally be, the reasons for trying some such new definition are easy enough to present.

In the first place, there may be many ways of making abstractions, and therefore many kinds of symbols. Abstraction is a process that allows of steps, incomplete phases, to which all sorts of protosymbolic phenomena, such as Cassirer adduces in his great *Philosophy of Symbolic Forms* (esp. Vol. II), might be related. Works of art, which I am sure have *import,* but not genuine *meaning,* are symbols of a sort, but not of the sort Nagel defined; for neither do they point beyond themselves to something thereafter known apart from the symbol, nor are they established by convention. It is their powerful articulation of form that enables us to perceive the form in its single instance. But they are, I think, quasi-symbols; they have some but not all the functions of genuine symbols. Melvin Rader suggested that one should speak of a work of art as an "expressive form" rather than as an "art symbol," and although I think the

2 For a further treatment of this problem, see "Emotion and Abstraction" (No. 4).

latter term perfectly defensible, I have used his term alternatively ever since.

Similar considerations apply to the dream elements which Freud classes as symbols. Surely they are not established by any convention; and although they are related to quite other ideas, which they are said to "mean," they are not in any usual sense employed to refer to those ideas. They do not denote them for the dreamer as words denote their objects. Yet the relation of dream figments to their meanings is one of *formulation* of the supposedly unconscious "dream thought," and in fact a rather complex abstraction of the emotional aspects of experiences; and the element common to symbol and "meaning" is a formal one—an abstract element.

Finally, the abstractive character of symbols is what gives them their scientific value. In science we have a highly developed special use of symbols, built on conventions, and resulting in the boldest abstractions that have ever been made. Scientific symbolization is, I think, always genuine *language,* in the strictest sense, and the symbolism of mathematics the greatest possible refinement of language; and language as such is the paradigm of symbolism, as its content—discursive thought—is of conception.

Whatever the difficulties of the proposed redefinition of "symbol," I think the direction is right; only a radical shift of approach can give us a basic concept elastic enough to allow the widely diverse definitions we want to derive, in essential relation to each other.

4 EMOTION AND ABSTRACTION

ABSTRACT THINKING, which is essential to any extensive course of reasoning, is traditionally treated as incompatible with emotional response. Cold reason and warm feeling (meaning emotion) are supposed to be antagonistic tendencies in the human mind, and people generally admire the one and trust its promptings, while they disparage and distrust the other. Religious mystics, many artists, and some philosophers in our own century, notably Bergson and his disciples, regard all abstract conception as an essential falsification of reality, and look to some inarticulate feeling, a product of instinct or intuition, to guide not only their practical behavior, but their knowledge of the nature of things. Scientists, educators, and analytic philosophers, perhaps also most men of affairs, take just the opposite stand, and hold abstract thought and cold reason—indeed, the colder the better—to be the safest guide to action and the arbiter of truth about a world of hard facts. They usually admit that their actions and even their beliefs are prone to follow the lures of feeling inspired by "the concrete situation" rather than the dictates of reason based on "abstract logic"; but that is because a certain amount of emotion inevitably interferes with one's logical thinking.

The antagonism between emotive responses and abstract ideation has become an accepted principle even among professional psychologists. Since reasoning—the prime use of such ideation—is regarded by most of them as an improved technique of getting food, safety, and sex partners, i.e., realizing the universal animal aims at a higher level, our spontaneous emotional reactions must be viewed as reversions to less suitable ways of dealing with the world and with each other; and they are, indeed, generally treated as disturbances of normal functions.[1] And even more than the behavioral psychologists, our rationally inclined epistemologists decry the influence of emotion on the working of other people's minds and on those people's resultant claims to knowledge. Such claims rest on "mere feeling," "wishful thinking," or what William James called "tender-mindedness," making concessions to sentiment; and, in the words of one of our contemporary analytic philosophers, they are "nothing more than the invisible shadows cast by emotive meaning." [2]

Those thinkers who, on the contrary, are deeply suspicious of the powers of reason, have to put something in its place as the cognitive and directive act of the mind. Their resort is usually to "instinct," which is supposed to be replaced at the human level by "intuition." As animal instincts express themselves in spontaneous "drives" to action, and produce great emotional symptoms if they are thwarted, so human intuition is experienced as an immediate feeling of certainty about the truth or falsehood of propositions, the rightness or wrongness of acts, and the nature of the unspoken thoughts and feelings of other people. Its chief theoretical virtue as a presumed mental faculty is its similarity to instinct, which makes it seem a little nearer than reason to most people's idea of "nature"; it is easier to imagine intuition as a higher form of instinct than to imagine the processes of generalization, deduction, and logical conclusion in that role. Actually, the shift from instinct to intuition is as hard to construe in terms of zoological development, i.e., evolution, as the shift from instinct to rationality. But the former seems simpler because it does not bring in the moot problem of abstraction. Intuitive knowledge of facts, like instinct, is bound to concrete situations; and to a great many minds "concrete" means "real," so that to them

[1] D. O. Hebb, in *The Organization of Behavior* (New York, 1949), considers emotion as a disruption of cortical organization (p. 148).

[2] C. I. Stevenson, "The Nature of Ethical Disagreement," in *Readings in Philosophical Analysis,* ed. by H. Feigl and W. Sellars (New York, 1949), p. 593.

intuition seems "nearer to reality" than thought, which manipulates abstract concepts and applies its "spectral dance of bloodless categories" to the real world. The protagonists of intuitive knowledge and instinctive guidance, whose greatest spokesman in modern European philosophy was Bergson, hold as he did that abstraction is a precarious and essentially unnatural artifice invented for practical purposes, but at the price of truth and genuine vital experience.

This tenet raises a grave question of human evolution. If abstraction is not a natural function, how was it ever invented? How was an act so foreign to animal mentality ever performed for the first time? We have various devices, accidentally discovered or deliberately designed, for making very rarefied and strained abstractions, which empower us to construct our admirable mathematics and rather terrifying science. But an artificial device is always essentially a real or intended improvement on natural means to an end, or a substitute for such means where they themselves fail (that is, a prosthesis). It may incidentally have an unforeseen effect which sets up a new purpose, as the invention of gunpowder was incidental to an alchemist's attempts to make gold, but once invented, production of gunpowder became the primary purpose of countless industrial artifices and techniques. These could never have been found, however, before the idea of an explosive substance had occurred to anyone; and if there had never been an explosion of any sort in human experience (e.g., in the course of a conflagration or volcanic upheaval), surely no one could have imagined such an event clearly enough to think of what we call "explosives," let alone seek or invent them. Similarly, the trick of abstract conception could never have been adopted for the sake of its practical advantages if it had not somehow occurred naturally in prehuman brains. It could only be put to practical use after it had evolved in the course of that cerebral specialization which made one primate genus become Man.

The question that invites our speculation (corroboration by factual findings being a sanguine hope at this stage) is, how the tendency to single out the salient features of experience that recur on different occasions or occur simultaneously in multiple instances, and to remember those features and recognize them as the same in each case, could have originated in a being that presumably was a pure animal when the process began. The use of concepts is the mark of human mentality; the earliest production of something like a concept must have resulted from the progressive development of activities that were natural and habitual to a high animal.

One of our besetting difficulties in forming hypotheses about the evolution of human traits is, I think, that we look for their origins in functions which served most nearly the same purposes. That is, however, to ignore a cardinal principle of biological advance, the shift of functions from one mechanism to another as the new one arises, and with that shift some entirely new goals to be attained.[3] Very often, moreover, an important purpose, such as for instance the balancing of the body, is served by several organic complexes, working on different principles[4]—older and newer structures sometimes coexisting, and able to stand in for each other under some, though seldom all, circumstances.[5] A new one becomes dominant because it has the greatest scope for elaboration. Had it not, we might never notice its existence, and there would be no radical shift from old ways of life to a new pattern.

Very high functions are usually composite in origin and await the development of necessary conditions, some of which, at a later stage, seem unessential or even inimical to them. Others, of course, are clearly recognizable in retrospect, and apt to be taken for "the cause." In the

[3] This principle has been recognized and largely explored by Arnold Gehlen in his valuable book *Der Mensch, seine Natur und seine Stellung in der Welt* (4th ed.; Bonn, 1950).

[4] Henri Piéron, in a paper entitled "Relations des receptions visuelles et labyrinthiques dans les réactions spatiales," *L' année psychol.*, LI (1949), 161–72, lists four different mechanisms of equilibration found in most mammals and some other animals, but of varying importance from species to species, and also, within each species and individual, from one situation to another.

[5] See, for example, J. G. Dusser de Barenne, " 'Corticalization' of Function and Functional Localization in the Cerebral Cortex," *Arch. Neurol. & Psychiat.*, XXX (1930), 884–901; see also K. S. Lashley, "The Problem of Cerebral Organization in Vision," in *Visual Mechanisms* (Lancaster, Pa., 1942), pp. 301–22.

case of abstract conception, the role of sensory specialization and of the consequent selection of stimuli by the highly specialized organs has long been recognized, since it resembles that of the selection or "taking out" of features from the welter of experience, which abstraction is supposed to be. In effect, of course, such a "taking out" does occur in fully developed conceptual abstraction; but it may have a different origin from that of what one might call "sensory abstraction," which has been seriously studied since the development of computing machines suggested some hypotheses that really seem to be fertile. The growing literature concerned with the mechanisms of abstractive vision and hearing is scattered over the fields of psychology, mathematics, small-current engineering, physiology, and neurology, but the ideas developed in these diverse fields are convergent. There is a good deal of evidence for the theory that the visual organ (which is easier to study than the auditory or tactual) has a function much like the "scanning" process of television instruments and some electron microscopes. According to Norbert Wiener, we can use and interpret line drawings because "somewhere in the visual process, outlines are emphasized and some other aspects of an image are minimized in importance. The beginning of the processes is in the eye itself." [6] For very plausible mechanical reasons, "the eye receives its most intense impression at boundaries, and . . . every visual image in fact has something of the nature of a line drawing." [7]

The emphasis on the outline here is produced by elimination of the "redundant" portions of the image, or "abstraction" in the purest classical sense; the process is automatically determined by the structure of the organ (not only the eye, but the whole optic tract, including the visual cortex), and the abstraction is performed unknown to its performer. On this hypothetical basis, Pitts and McCulloch have worked out a further theory of intellectual abstraction briefly presented in an article entitled,

[6] *Cybernetics, or Control and Communication in the Animal and the Machine* (New York, 1948), p. 156.
[7] *Ibid.*, p. 159.

"How We Know Universals." [8] It is most reasonable, of course, on finding an abstractive function of eye and ear, to explore the possibilities of analogous processes in other highly developed parts of the central nervous system, which might furnish a theory of further cognitive mechanisms. Yet the account in the above-mentioned paper somehow does not fulfill the promise in the title, although the explanation rings true enough as far as it goes. It seems not to go far enough, but to stop somewhere short of explaining the genesis of human conception. One is left with the question: What is missing?

What is missing is the recognition of a difference between the way we form "universals" and the way we know them. The analogy between the hypothetical processes in the sensory mechanisms and the more elaborate and variable ones in the "interpretive cortex" serves to explain the element of pattern recognition that is evinced in the behavior of animals. As Russell Brain said, it is essential to their survival that they should recognize not only a specific thing or creature again, but any other of the same sort; and, indeed, "what the animal reacts to is not a mosaic of all the individual features of the object perceived, but a pattern which constitutes an abstraction from any particular individual, but for that reason is common to all individuals of the group." [9] This sort of abstraction, however, is still what Bouissou has called "abstraction implicite"; [10] it is a selective response on the organic level, but not on a conceptual one. And Sir Russell makes a very precise statement when he says, "Pitts and McCulloch have attempted to describe in mathematical terms the physiological processes in virtue of which the brain renders possible the recognition of universals." [11]

[8] Walter Pitts and W. S. McCulloch, "How We Know Universals: The Perception of Auditory and Visual Forms," *Bull. Math. Biophys.*, IX (1947), 127–47. See also W. S. McCulloch and W. Pitts, "The Statistical Organization of Nervous Activity," *Biometrics*, IV (1948), 91–99.

[9] "The Cerebral Basis of Consciousness," *Brain*, LXXIII (1950), 465–79; see esp. p. 471.

[10] René Bouissou, *Essai sur l'abstraction et son rôle dans la connaissance* (1942), p. 55.

[11] *Op. cit.*, p. 472.

These processes—be they like scanning and "seeking" techniques in our machines, or not—are undoubtedly necessary for the making of abstract concepts, but not sufficient. They may, indeed, make conception possible, yet to make it actual requires something more. That further element, I maintain, is emotional.

The only functions which can be granted to emotion in a computer animal are those of sustaining attention and acting as an "overdrive" to action in emergency. If our mental superiority to the Metazoa were a direct and simple result of more and more formalized responses to more and more filtered, fused, and automatically generalized perceptual stimuli, then the strength of our emotions, which far exceeds the requirements of those functions, would certainly not exemplify the principles of economy that the organism (apparently devising itself with more forethought than it will ever have again) is supposed to observe in its designs.[12] Were our rationality purely an increase of automatic processes instead of a new development supervening on such an increase, emotions would really be the sheer disturbances they are often taken to be, atavistic responses disrupting practical behavior, and the continued toleration of such monkey wrenches in an exemplary self-preservation machine would be an evolutionary curiosity. Animals, living as they do from one emergency to another, need terror to put speed into their escapes or to "freeze" them into invisibility for motion-seeking eyes, because they cannot figure out strategies or gauge the best goal for a retreat. They need the intense excitement of the hunt to keep them on the trail past momentary discouragements by obstacles or disappearance of the quarry.[13] Men can or-

---

[12] Cf. Wiener, *op. cit.*, p. 155: "There should be some parts of the apparatus . . . which will search for free components and connectors of the various sorts of combinations and allot them as they are needed. This will eliminate . . . expense which is due to having a great number of unused elements, which cannot be used unless their entire large assembly is used." And below: "The blood leaving the brain is a fraction of a degree warmer than that entering it. No other computing machine approaches the economy of energy of the brain."

[13] Hans Jonas has developed this idea in "Motility and Emotion: An Essay in Philosophical Biology," *Proceedings of the Eleventh International Congress of Philosophy* (1953), Vol. VII, pp. 117–22.

ganize a hunt long in advance, and gather for it with or without enthusiasm, if it is necessary to fill the larder while the game is running or while other affairs permit. Yet most animals seem to be indifferent when no exciting situation evokes their emotions, while human beings generally exhibit some degree of elation or gloom, readiness to be touched in one way or another by everything around them; and the waves of feeling elicited by trivial events are greater than any practical response requires, especially where the most appropriate behavior is to desist from any overt action.

The rise of human mentality from animal mentality rests, I think, on one of those shifts of functions from old to new mechanisms which occur as the old ones develop to their limit of complexity and refinement, the point of physiological overelaboration and overresponsiveness. In the human brain, the cortical structures which we currently hold responsible for the automatic abstraction of formal features from experience are certainly developed far beyond those in any other brains. Professor Wiener, in fact, proposed that the human cortex has already exceeded its most serviceable degree of complication, and that its continued overgrowth must finally lead the human species to extinction.[14] If a phylogenetic tendency always continued to its own highest realization at the expense of the organism as a whole, this prediction would carry great weight. But unlimited phylogenetic progressions are rare. The armored saurians, the dodo, and a few other extinct creatures are supposed to have become unviable through their exaggerated specialties; usually, however, such excesses are not reached. When an organ becomes too elaborate, so that the minutiae of its performance begin to cancel or block each other, these detailed acts may be replaced by a simpler function of some new mechanism, or else fall under the influence of another, separately developed organ, so that the joint operation constitutes a higher function serving the same vital ends. If human brains continued to work as animal brains, only with ever-increasing generality of perception and ever-widening transfer of responses, we

14 *Op. cit.*, p. 180.

might really be outdoing ourselves in filtering out details, and ignore too many cues for quick extempore response. But human beings do not depend to a very great
extent on short-range direct responses, because their
chief stock in trade is a tremendous store of symbols—
images, words, and fragmentary presentations without
clear identity, but with meaning—which can be manipulated independently of current stimuli from the environment. At an advanced stage of symbolic activity such
manipulation goes on almost all the time, either as reflec-
tive judging, predicting, and planning, or as free imagination, fiction, dramatic fancy, and—most effectively—
new abstract formulation of facts, i.e., interpretation. This
sort of thing does not result from filtering and scanning,
or consist in making response combinations appropriate
to a stimulus situation. Symbolic activity arises mainly
from within the organism, especially from within the brain
itself.

The cortical functions indubitably are not the only
ones which have undergone great elaboration in the
course of our rise from animal to human estate; all parts
of the brain have changed, and their massive responses
have split up into distinct and separately evocable acts.
Emotions, too, have become articulated, and each impulse spends itself somewhere in the system. While
formerly a strong perceptual stimulus would always throw
the whole creature into overt action and a simple emotive
state, our many percepts instantly touch off several different cerebral acts, which no longer summate to produce
one total behavioral response, but terminate each in a
moment of emotion which meets and cathects the act of
perception, recall, expectation, or whatever else that induced it. Since the expression of one emotion is often
incompatible with that of another, and yet the kaleidoscopic passage of events around and within us stirs
feelings of every sort all the time, most of these emotive
processes are cut off from overt expression and have to
spend themselves within the brain. We do not know just
how their tiny courses run, any more than we know
the whole career of a perceptual act; but the centrally
based emotion seems to be carried along with the perception that started it, and is shaped in its progress by the

forms which automatic sensory abstraction has already prepared. This gives the "emotional charge" to forms which may recur; and since these forms may recur in events which are otherwise new, the cathexis, too slight to be called anything more than "interest" or even "notice," belongs to some common formal features of various percepts, memories, and even expectations, and lends them a different sort of emphasis from that which the perceptual apparatus itself provided.

The abstraction inherent in perception as such results (if our current theories are right) from the elimination of countless possible stimuli; so the simplification is effected as in a lithograph, by eliminating everything but the features that will be left to function. It is not a process of emphasizing anything, but essentially of simplifying, lightening the load before its impact on the nervous system has gone very far. This process is not usually felt. The emotive act, on the other hand, is really an act of emphasizing the exciting features, and is an act that is felt, even if only as awareness of them; it may enhance the original simplification or make a new one, even several new ones by turns, and yield the well-known phenomena of changing gestalt. In this process the irrelevant material is not filtered out, but eclipsed by the intensification of the great lines.[15] Consequently the form seems to emerge from a rich background of vaguer details that may attain varying degrees of importance, and it may be their fluctuation which makes the stable lines strong by contrast.

When forms of perception coincide with forms of emotion, percepts themselves become emotive symbols. That is, of course, a large and mainly speculative subject beyond consideration here. The attainment of symbolic value apparently antedates the final stage of real conceptual thought, which grows up only with language; so there is a phase of formal intuition and implicit meaning

[15] This may be what Anton Ehrenzweig, in *The Psychoanalysis of Artistic Vision and Hearing* (London, 1953), p. 15, calls "Structural Repression." If so, "repression" is not a good designation; "neglect" would be better. But I am not at all sure that we conceive the process in the same way, or even refer to the same phenomenon.

in the evolution of symbolism that may go further back
in history than the phase I would call explicit abstraction,
the basis of genuine conceptual thinking.[16] It is only in
the phase of explicit abstraction that thought becomes a
self-contained systematic process, by which attention is
focused on highly refined forms extrapolated from experience, by virtue of a symbolism which has so little emotional value of its own that the form it exemplifies is
its only possible point of interest. Specially restricted
words, or marks on paper, are the most convenient
symbols for long trains of reasoning; all richer exempli-
fications of concepts present irrelevant aspects which
may receive extraneous emotional emphasis and confuse
the abstracted concept.

Such undesired emphasis comes from the fact that in
human life practically every detail of memory or current impression has its own emotional charge: that is to
say, our emotive responses are as capable of differentiation as our perceptive ones. Experiments have shown
the degree to which our cortical processes are indi-
vidually cathected, and either facilitated or obstructed
(though often as briefly as 0.01 sec.) by their particular
cathexis.[17] There is, then, a play of felt processes arising
from the deeper structures of the central nervous system,
as well as a play of impressions; and the production of
images, explicit memories, and conceptual elements
probably takes place when the automatic formulations

[16] Implicit abstraction and implicit meaning reach a high development in art, where they are recognized by artistic intuition,
so-called "artistic sensibility," or not at all. The subject is too
great to be treated in passing, but is touched on in "The Cultural
Importance of Art" (No. 5), and discussed more fully in three essays: "Expressiveness," "Living Form," and "Abstraction in Science and Abstraction in Art," in *Problems of Art* (New York,
1956), as well as in the early chapters of *Feeling and Form* (New
York, 1953).

[17] There is a growing literature in this field, of which I mention only an obvious example, the work of Jerome Bruner with
various collaborators: J. S. Bruner and C. C. Goodman, "Need
and Value as Organizing Factors in Perception," *J. Abnormal &
Social Psychol.*, XLII (1947), 33–44; L. Postman, J. S. Bruner,
and E. McGinnies, "Personal Values as Selective Factors in Perception," *J. Abnormal & Social Psychol.*, XLIII (1948), 142–54;
J. S. Bruner and L. Postman, "Tension and Tension-Release as
Organizing Factors in Perception," *J. Personality*, XV (1947),
300–308.

made by the sense organs and cortical neurone assemblies are utilized as channels for discharge of the rapid emotive responses made to those sensory and cortical acts themselves.

With the growth of perceptual and so-called "associational" activity in the human brain, events in psychical phase may well have become so numerous that behavior was confused by the welter of great and small feelings and lures to attention; and we should perhaps have already succumbed to the overdevelopment and overcomplication which Professor Wiener foresees as our fate, were it not for the fact that the new faculty of formal abstraction, and a still further one of symbolic thinking, have furnished means of completing countless induced processes very quickly, in a purely intracerebral way. At the same time, these new mechanisms which relieve the excessive pressures of conflicting emotions have greatly reduced the importance of those animal actions for which the brain is becoming uneconomically complex, because they perform equivalent actions on quite different principles. With the advent of abstract conception and conceptual thinking there has been a shift of functions all along the line, from intelligent behavior to intellect, from universal responses[18] to knowledge of universals, from animal mentality to the human mind.

If it is true that explicit abstraction is made by the joint functions of perceptual and emotional mechanisms, when these both reach the point where their differentiations become so fine that noticeable effects usually require summation of impulses, we are faced with the paradoxical finding that only a highly emotional creature could have developed the talent of abstract thought. At some period in our prehuman history the pressure of central excitements must have become so great that if the countless impulses started by the increasing cortical action had continued to commingle and break through to massive overt expression, the animal's behavior would have become disrupted. The only internal adaptation to the over-

[18] I here use the term "universal" because McCulloch, Pitts, and other scientists use it to mean what logicians would call "general" (subsuming "universal" and "particular"), and sometimes to mean what is more strictly called "abstract," i.e., purely formal.

growing sensory mechanisms and their dependencies was to spend the emotional impulses aroused by their individuated acts in equally piecemeal fashion; and as it often happens, the very changes that caused the crisis offered the means of surviving it. The separate intellectual processes took up the separate central impulses they evoked, and the extra charge this gave them raised their automatically simplified main forms, and these only, to the psychical level. The conscious processes that resulted—images, gestures, explicit memories, and other mental phenomena—provided the material for the final humanizing function, the use of symbols.

It is not impossible that mankind has passed through a much more emotional phase than it exhibits at present, a time when survival really hung in the balance. The function of symbolization, which is so deeply rooted in our brains that it begins spontaneously in infant experience and in dream, spends much of our central response. The most primitive symbols—the "archetypes," as Dr. Jung called them—still show a surcharge of emotion that may have belonged to all symbols, before they so proliferated that the whole mental life was somewhat intellectualized and the pressure for purely self-expressive overt action was reduced. It is interesting to note that the animals nearest to man in the evolutionary scale, the great apes, are much more easily frenzied or reduced to cataleptic collapse by emotional stimuli than human beings. Are they at the end of their tether in the realm of animal mentation? There are indications in their behavior that they may be near the threshold of fantasy, the preparation for thought. But this thought may be too close to fantasy itself; so perhaps it had better be left alone.

5 THE CULTURAL IMPORTANCE OF ART*

EVERY CULTURE develops some kind of art as surely as it develops language. Some primitive cultures have no real mythology or religion, but all have some art—dance, song, design (sometimes only on tools or on the human body). Dance, above all, seems to be the oldest elaborated art.

The ancient ubiquitous character of art contrasts sharply with the prevalent idea that art is a luxury product of civilization, a cultural frill, a piece of social veneer.

It fits better with the conviction held by most artists, that art is the epitome of human life, the truest record of insight and feeling, and that the strongest military or economic society without art is poor in comparison with the most primitive tribe of savage painters, dancers, or idol carvers. Wherever a society has really achieved culture (in the ethnological sense, not the popular sense of "social form") it has begotten art, not late in its career, but at the very inception of it.

Art is, indeed, the spearhead of human development, social and individual. The vulgarization of art is the surest symptom of ethnic decline. The growth of a new art or even a great and radically new style always bespeaks a young and vigorous mind, whether collective or single.

What sort of thing is art, that it should play such a

* A lecture delivered at Syracuse University; reprinted from *Aesthetic Form and Education*, ed. M. F. Andrews, Syracuse, N. Y., 1958.

leading role in human development? It is not an intellectual pursuit, but is necessary to intellectual life; it is
not religion, but grows up with religion, serves it, and
in large measure determines it.

We cannot enter here on a long discussion of what
has been claimed as the essence of art, the true nature
of art, or its defining function; in a single lecture dealing with one aspect of art, namely its cultural influence,
I can only give you by way of preamble my own definition of art, with categorical brevity. This does not mean
that I set up this definition in a categorical spirit, but
only that we have no time to debate it; so you are asked
to accept it as an assumption underlying these reflections.

Art, in the sense here intended—that is, the generic
term subsuming painting, sculpture, architecture, music,
dance, literature, drama, and film—may be defined as
the practice of creating perceptible forms expressive of
human feeling. I say "perceptible" rather than "sensuous" forms because some works of art are given to
imagination rather than to the outward senses. A novel,
for instance, usually is read silently with the eye, but is
not made for vision, as a painting is; and though sound
plays a vital part in poetry, words even in poetry are
not essentially sonorous structures like music. Dance
requires to be seen, but its appeal is to deeper centers
of sensation. The difference between dance and mobile
sculpture makes this immediately apparent. But all
works of art are purely perceptible forms that seem to
embody some sort of feeling.

"Feeling" as I am using it here covers much more
than it does in the technical vocabulary of psychology,
where it denotes only pleasure and displeasure, or even
in the shifting limits of ordinary discourse, where it
sometimes means sensation (as when one says a para-
lyzed limb has no feeling in it), sometimes sensibility
(as we speak of hurting someone's feelings), sometimes
emotion (e.g., as a situation is said to harrow your feelings, or to evoke tender feeling), or a directed emotional attitude (we say we feel strongly *about* something), or even our general mental or physical condition, feeling well or ill, blue, or a bit above ourselves.

As I use the word, in defining art as the creation of perceptible forms expressive of human feeling, it takes in all those meanings; it applies to everything that may be felt.

Another word in the definition that might be questioned is "creation." I think it is justified, not pretentious, as perhaps it sounds, but that issue is slightly beside the point here; so let us shelve it. If anyone prefers to speak of the "making" or "construction" of expressive forms, that will do here just as well.

What does have to be understood is the meaning of "form," and more particularly "expressive form"; for that involves the very nature of art and therefore the question of its cultural importance.

The word "form" has several current uses; most of them have some relation to the sense in which I am using it here, though a few, such as "a form to be filled in for tax purposes" or "a mere matter of form," are fairly remote, being quite specialized. Since we are speaking of art, it might be good to point out that the meaning of stylistic pattern—"the sonata form," "the sonnet form"—is not the one I am assuming here.

I am using the word in a simpler sense, which it has when you say, on a foggy night, that you see dimly moving forms in the mist; one of them emerges clearly, and is the form of a man. The trees are gigantic forms; the rills of rain trace sinuous forms on the windowpane. The rills are not fixed things; they are forms of motion. When you watch gnats weaving in the air, or flocks of birds wheeling overhead, you see dynamic forms— forms made by motion.

It is in this sense of an apparition given to our perception that a work of art is a form. It may be a permanent form like a building or a vase or a picture, or a transient, dynamic form like a melody or a dance, or even a form given to imagination, like the passage of purely imaginary, apparent events that constitutes a literary work. But it is always a perceptible, self-identical whole; like a natural being, it has a character of organic unity, self-sufficiency, individual reality. And it is thus, as an appearance, that a work of art is good or bad or perhaps only rather poor—as an appearance, not as a comment on things beyond it in the world, or as a reminder of them.

This, then, is what I mean by "form"; but what is meant by calling such forms "expressive of human feeling"? How do apparitions "express" anything—feeling or anything else? First of all, let us ask just what is meant here by "express," what sort of "expression" we are talking about.

The word "expression" has two principal meanings. In one sense it means self-expression—giving vent to our feelings. In this sense it refers to a symptom of what we feel. Self-expression is a spontaneous reaction to an actual, present situation, an event, the company we are in, things people say, or what the weather does to us; it bespeaks the physical and mental state we are in and the emotions that stir us.

In another sense, however, "expression" means the presentation of an idea, usually by the proper and apt use of words. But a device for presenting an idea is what we call a symbol, not a symptom. Thus a word is a symbol, and so is a meaningful combination of words.

A sentence, which is a special combination of words, expresses the idea of some state of affairs, real or imagined. Sentences are complicated symbols. Language will formulate new ideas as well as communicate old ones, so that all people know a lot of things that they have merely heard or read about. Symbolic expression, therefore, extends our knowledge beyond the scope of our actual experience.

If an idea is clearly conveyed by means of symbols we say it is well expressed. A person may work for a long time to give his statement the best possible form, to find the exact words for what he means to say, and to carry his account or his argument most directly from one point to another. But a discourse so worked out is certainly not a spontaneous reaction. Giving expression to an idea is obviously a different thing from giving expression to feelings. You do not say of a man in a rage that his anger is well expressed. The symptoms just are what they are; there is no critical standard for symptoms. If, on the other hand, the angry man tries to tell you what he is fuming about, he will have to collect himself, curtail his emotional expression, and find words to express his ideas. For to tell a story coherently involves "expression" in quite a different sense: this sort of expression is not "self-expression," but may be called "conceptual expression."

Language, of course, is our prime instrument of conceptual expression. The things we can say are in effect the things we can think. Words are the terms of our thinking as well as the terms in which we present our thoughts, because they present the objects of thought to the thinker himself. Before language communicates ideas, it gives them form, makes them clear, and in fact makes them what they are. Whatever has a name is an object for thought. Without words, sense experience is only a flow of impressions, as subjective as our feelings; words make it objective, and carve it up into *things* and *facts* that we can note, remember, and think about. Language gives outward experience its form, and makes it definite and clear.

There is, however, an important part of reality that is quite inaccessible to the formative influence of language: that is the realm of so-called "inner experience," the life of feeling and emotion. The reason why language is so powerless here is not, as many people suppose, that feeling and emotion are irrational; on the contrary, they seem irrational because language does not help to make them conceivable, and most people cannot conceive anything without the logical scaffolding of words. The unfitness of language to convey subjective experience is a somewhat technical subject, easier for logicians to understand than for artists; but the gist of it is that the form of language does not reflect the natural form of feeling, so that we cannot shape any extensive concepts of feeling with the help of ordinary, discursive language. Therefore the words whereby we refer to feeling only name very general kinds of inner experience—excitement, calm, joy, sorrow, love, hate, and so on. But there is no language to describe just how one joy differs, sometimes radically, from another. The real nature of feeling is something language as such—as discursive symbolism—cannot render.

For this reason, the phenomena of feeling and emotion are usually treated by philosophers as irrational. The only pattern discursive thought can find in them is the pattern of outward events that occasion them. There are different degrees of fear, but they are thought of as so many degrees of the same simple feeling.

But human feeling is a fabric, not a vague mass. It has an intricate dynamic pattern, possible combinations and new emergent phenomena. It is a pattern of organically interdependent and interdetermined tensions and resolutions, a pattern of almost infinitely complex activation and cadence. To it belongs the whole gamut of our sensibility—the sense of straining thought, all mental attitude and motor set. Those are the deeper reaches that underlie the surface waves of our emotion, and make human life a life of feeling instead of an unconscious metabolic existence interrupted by feelings.

It is, I think, this dynamic pattern that finds its formal expression in the arts. The expressiveness of art is like that of a symbol, not that of an emotional symptom; it is as a formulation of feeling for our conception that a work of art is properly said to be expressive. It may serve somebody's need of self-expression besides, but that is not what makes it good or bad art. In a special sense one may call a work of art a symbol of feeling, for, like a symbol, it formulates our ideas of inward experience, as discourse formulates our ideas of things and facts in the outside world. A work of art differs from a genuine symbol—that is, a symbol in the full and usual sense—in that it does not point beyond itself to something else. Its relation to feeling is a rather special one that we cannot undertake to analyze here; in effect, the feeling it expresses appears to be directly given with it —as the sense of a true metaphor, or the value of a religious myth—and is not separable from its expression. We speak of the feeling *of,* or the feeling *in,* a work of art, not the feeling it means. And we speak truly; a work of art presents something like a direct vision of vitality, emotion, subjective reality.

The primary function of art is to objectify feeling so that we can contemplate and understand it. It is the formulation of so-called "inward experience," the "inner life," that is impossible to achieve by discursive thought, because its forms are incommensurable with the forms of language and all its derivatives (e.g., mathematics, symbolic logic). Art objectifies the sentience and desire, self-consciousness and world-consciousness, emotions and moods, that are generally regarded as irrational because words cannot give us clear ideas of them. But the premise tacitly assumed in such a judgment— namely, that anything language cannot express is formless and irrational—seems to me to be an error. I believe the life of feeling is not irrational; its logical forms are merely very different from the structures of discourse. But they are so much like the dynamic forms of art that art is their natural symbol. Through plastic works, music, fiction, dance, or dramatic forms we can conceive what vitality and emotion feel like.

This brings us, at last, to the question of the cultural importance of the arts. Why is art so apt to be the vanguard of cultural advance, as it was in Egypt, in Greece, in Christian Europe (think of Gregorian music and Gothic architecture), in Renaissance Italy—not to speculate about ancient cavemen, whose art is all that we know of them? One thinks of culture as economic increase, social organization, the gradual ascendancy of rational thinking and scientific control of nature over superstitious imagination and magical practices. But art is not practical; it is neither philosophy nor science; it is not religion, morality, or even social comment (as many drama critics take comedy to be). What does it contribute to culture that could be of major importance?

It merely presents forms—sometimes intangible forms —to imagination. Its direct appeal is to that faculty, or function, that Lord Bacon considered the chief stumbling block in the way of reason, and that enlightened writers like Stuart Chase never tire of condemning as the source of all nonsense and bizarre erroneous beliefs. And so it is; but it is also the source of all insight and true beliefs. Imagination is probably the oldest mental trait that is typically human—older than discursive reason; it is probably the common source of dream, reason, religion, and all true general observation. It is this primitive human power—imagination—that engenders the arts and is in turn directly affected by their products.

Somewhere at the animalian starting line of human evolution lie the beginnings of that supreme instrument of the mind—language. We think of it as a device for communication among the members of a society. But communication is only one, and perhaps not even the first, of its functions. The first thing it does is to break up what William James called the "blooming, buzzing confusion" of sense perception into units and groups, events and chains of events—things and relations, causes and effects. All these patterns are imposed on our experience by language. We think, as we speak, in terms of objects and their relations.

But the process of breaking up our sense experience in this way, making reality conceivable, memorable, sometimes even predictable, is a process of imagination. Primitive conception is imagination. Language and imagination grow up together in a reciprocal tutelage.

What discursive symbolism—language in its literal use —does for our awareness of things about us and our own relation to them, the arts do for our awareness of subjective reality, feeling and emotion; they give form to inward experiences and thus make them conceivable. The only way we can really envisage vital movement, the stirring and growth and passage of emotion, and ultimately the whole direct sense of human life, is in artistic terms. A musical person thinks of emotions musically. They cannot be discursively talked about above a very general level. But they may nonetheless be known—objectively set forth, publicly known—and there is nothing necessarily confused or formless about emotions.

As soon as the natural forms of subjective experience are abstracted to the point of symbolic presentation, we can use those forms to imagine feeling and understand its nature. Self-knowledge, insight into all phases of life and mind, springs from artistic imagination. That is the cognitive value of the arts.

But their influence on human life goes deeper than the intellectual level. As language actually gives form to our sense experience, grouping our impressions around those things which have names, and fitting sensations to the qualities that have adjectival names, and so on, the arts we live with—our picture books and stories and the music we hear—actually form our emotive experience. Every generation has its styles of feeling. One age shudders and blushes and faints, another swaggers, still another is godlike in a universal indifference. These styles in actual emotion are not insincere. They are largely unconscious—determined by many social causes, but *shaped* by artists, usually popular artists of the screen, the jukebox, the shop-window, and the picture magazine. (That, rather than incitement to crime, is my objection to the comics.) Irwin Edman remarks in one of his books that our emotions are largely Shakespeare's poetry.

This influence of art on life gives us an indication of why a period of efflorescence in the arts is apt to lead a cultural advance: it formulates a new way of feeling, and that is the beginning of a cultural age. It suggests another matter for reflection, too—that a wide neglect of artistic education is a neglect in the education of feeling. Most people are so imbued with the idea that feeling is a formless, total organic excitement in men as in animals that the idea of educating feeling, developing its scope and quality, seems odd to them, if not absurd. It is really, I think, at the very heart of personal education.

There is one other function of the arts that benefits not so much the advance of culture as its stabilization —an influence on individual lives. This function is the converse and complement of the objectification of feeling, the driving force of creation in art: it is the education of vision that we receive in seeing, hearing, reading works of art—the development of the artist's eye, that assimilates ordinary sights (or sounds, motions, or events) to inward vision, and lends expressiveness and emotional import to the world. Wherever art takes a motif from actuality—a flowering branch, a bit of landscape, a historic event, or a personal memory, any model or theme from life—it transforms it into a piece of imagination, and imbues its image with artistic vitality. The result is an impregnation of ordinary reality with the significance of created form. This is the subjectification of nature that makes reality itself a symbol of life and feeling.

The arts objectify subjective reality, and subjectify outward experience of nature. Art education is the education of feeling, and a society that neglects it gives itself up to formless emotion. Bad art is corruption of feeling. This is a large factor in the irrationalism which dictators and demagogues exploit.

6 SCIENTIFIC CIVILIZATION AND CULTURAL CRISIS*

EVERY HUMAN LIFE has an undercurrent of feeling that is peculiar to it. Each individual expresses this continuous pattern of feeling in what we call his "personality," reflected in behavior, speech, voice, and even physical bearing (stance and walk) as his *individual style*. On a larger scale, every human society has its undercurrent of feeling which is not individual, but general. Every person shares in it to some degree, and develops his own life of feeling within the frame of the style prevailing in his country and his time.

Almost everywhere in the world today, the undercurrent of feeling is confused, uncertain, strained. There is much pride in it, but under the pride, fear; a great faith in science, and at the same time an irrationalism which betrays the shakiness of such faith; a growing sense of world society, human rights, and the equal dignity of all mankind, and yet a prevailing hostility and jealousy that makes the world's political pattern a protracted "cold war," in which every society eventually becomes involved. The basic feeling of most people today seems to be one of deep confusion in morals, aims, values, beliefs, and motives.

The reason for all this emotional instability is not hard to find. Our generation has seen the greatest, most spectacular change of the human scene that has ever been recorded in history. It started with the so-called "industrial revolution" in Europe—the invention of power-

* This paper was presented at a meeting of the Japan Association for Philosophy of Science at Nikko, Japan, in August 1961.

driven machines to do the work that hands had always done, which led to mass production of goods. Mass production had the most dramatic effects on European civilization, making it boom into an entirely new way of life, and spread the economy and the political sway of Europe, briefly at least, over oceans and continents, especially westward to America, so that today the two American continents are European in language and largely in population. When I speak of "modern civilization," therefore, I mean this civilization which has emanated from Europe, and found little to stop it from establishing itself first in America, and gradually throughout the world. Whatever it found it usually swamped and sank, as past civilizations undoubtedly did in their day.

It is only rather recently that we are realizing what it has destroyed, and also the very grave fact that in its advance it is still destroying many things of undoubted and irreplaceable value—social orders of rank and status built up by a long national or local history, religious faith and its institutions, arts supported by solid and good traditions, ways of life in which people have long felt secure and useful. Such losses are not to be taken lightly.

There is no denying that the spearhead of this ruthless social revolution is something we all—at least in our present gathered company—honor and desire: science. Science is the source and the pacemaker of this modern civilization which is sweeping away a whole world of cultural values. It is with good reason that we are meeting here to discuss the role of science in civilization; I would like to carry the issue a little further, and talk about the effect of this scientific civilization on human culture throughout the contemporary world. For it is not only in countries on which it has impinged suddenly and dramatically, but also in the countries of its origin— in Europe and America—that the technological revolution, with its entirely new mental and material standards, has deeply disturbed local and even national cultures.

This observation has a certain air of paradox. How can civilization kill culture? Are not civilization and culture the same thing?

Wherever we encounter a paradox, we may look for a

philosophical problem—that is, for a problem of meaning. Philosophy is the systematic study of meanings. Paradoxes are engendered by inexact or incomplete definitions, and a closer study of the concepts involved in them usually removes the paradoxes and reveals interesting distinctions among closely related processes and conditions instead. So the question which confronts us is essentially what we mean by culture and what by civilization. A more precise understanding of these two terms may serve to explain how, despite their intimate connection, a great strain may arise between a rapidly growing civilization and cultural values.

That civilization and culture are not the same thing is evident in the fact that there may be savage or civilized cultures. "Savage civilization," however, is a contradiction in terms.

A culture is the symbolic expression of developed habitual ways of feeling. By "feeling" I do not mean particularly pleasure and displeasure, to which many psychologists limit the word, or just emotion and sensation, but *everything that can be felt.* We feel such elusive things as rhythms of attention and the strain of thought, bodily relaxation or tension that cannot be reduced to any particular sensation, attitudes of mind, the general activity of our imagination, confidence in the goodness of life, or fundamental annoyance, boredom, cynicism, or again the countless modes of humor. Humor is one of the most individual marks of a people. All such phenomena of sensibility and general emotivity I am subsuming here under the word "feeling," as well as the distinct emotions. By *ways* of feeling I mean the degree to which feelings are apt to go, their persistence or transience, the quickness of various responses, and their directedness to certain events rather than others.

Culture is the expression of this characteristic pattern of feeling, which sets one people off from another, in the pattern of their actions and the things involved in their actions—that is, specifically *their* things. Acts are generally purposive, and things useful, i.e., serving purposes; but both acts and artifacts go beyond practical needs in that they take on formal character, which is not efficacious, but expressive. Human movements are not only

motivated actions, but also gestures; human objects—
from toothpicks to houses, cars, ships—have not only
uses, but also *style*. The element of gesture in our actions
is their gradual, unconscious, or deliberate and conscious
formalization. This is most pronounced and detailed in
ritual—religious, military, academic, or purely festive—
especially, of course, religious, which is often quite intentionally symbolic of personal attitudes and aided by
more permanent symbols, cult objects and images. Yet
ritual is by no means the whole field of formalized action;
some gestic value accrues to practically all social behavior as propriety, taste, good speech or coarse speech,
good or bad manners, conformity or departure from un-
stated but familiar norms.

Such objective formal channels of personal expression
are our social heritage; and as they lend our feelings and
attitudes expression, they also shape and establish them.
They are the public influences which acculturate our private lives, and guarantee the continuity of vital feeling
that unifies a natural community. Morality, custom, and
religion are, therefore, essentially conservative; and if
they are left unshaken for very long periods they always
harbor the danger of becoming ossified so that feeling is
reduced and devitalized in their narrowing channels. A
growing culture requires departure, change, novelty in
expressive forms—in language and ideas, visible objects,
ways of doing things. There has to be a creative advance
at fairly brief intervals, if not all the time. Pioneering is
the work of individuals, and a culture is doomed if it does
not produce great nonconformists, who break the inherited molds of expression by the force of their own
new ideas, which cut a channel for new elements of feeling
and carve out a frame for new attitudes and moral senti-
ments.

Such personal innovations, however, may also be
handed down from the very great to lesser men, or to
younger people of genius as a cultural legacy. Culture is
the entire treasure of achievement in a society. Its advance is somewhat like organic growth, slow, cumulative,
changing, yet self-identical.

Civilization is a somewhat different phenomenon. It is
always a product of a high culture; but instead of being

the symbolic aspect of behavior, it is the pattern of the practical implementation of life—practical, not necessarily physical. Such arrangements as contracts, liabilities, legal regulations (e.g., traffic rules) are not physical instruments, but they are purely symbolic—pieces of paper, oystershell, metal, or what not. And their aim is to facilitate the conduct of life.

Civilization, as the word implies, comes with the rise of cities. It is essentially a product of city life, and spreads from urban centers to the country. As long as a population lives directly on the land, each family finds or raises its own food, builds its own domicile, and perhaps hands it on from one generation to another; public decisions are made by direct discussion, vote, declaration, command, or whatever the practice; goods are exchanged directly between interested parties. Custom usually suffices to determine people's duties and rights, and judges rely on it in deciding cases of wrongdoing or conflicts of interests. But when people cluster together in cities this ancient pattern breaks down. They can no longer hunt or raise their own food; the countryside has to supply it, day by day. They cannot offer goods in exchange for it, because they have nothing to offer that the food raisers or gatherers require day by day, so a medium of exchange becomes necessary—money. With money, commerce becomes too complicated to be conducted on a basis of customary practices; besides, people in cities are often gathered from different communities, with various customs. This makes statute law necessary. An important *cultural* contribution of civic life is the close contact of people with each other, which steps up the exchange of ideas, the chance for each individual to learn things beyond his experience and ancestral background, the ferment of novelty contrasting with the quiet repetitiousness of country life. There is a change in mentality. Also, the city provides a goal of travel; communication and movement assume a new importance. Everything tends toward the historic phenomenon we call "civilization"—the practical organization of life, public and private.

The seeds of civilization are in every culture, but it is city life that brings them to fruition. Like every process of fruition, civilization strains and drains the life which engenders and supports it—the culture which reaches its height in this development. Civilized life establishes a new balance between conservative and progressive elements, and tips the scales of feeling toward the venturesome, personalistic pole and away from piety and decorum. Such a shift of balance does not take place, of course, without flagrant exhibits of complete imbalance —lives culturally lost, degenerated, the familiar "criminal elements" and irresponsible drifters of every big city in the world.

This in itself, however, would probably not throw a great and prosperous culture into crisis; even the growing adventurousness of urban mentality, which leads the community to aggression, wars of conquest, organized command, perhaps wide-flung empire, need not be fundamentally disturbing. Cultures have been built around war, and expressed themselves in feats and triumphs and trophies. The danger of civilization to cultural life, more acute in our own world than in any previous era, is something less awful-looking, but really more serious. It has changed the character and the very function of war itself.

It is simply the fact that civilization can be transplanted, and live apart from its cultural roots. It can be grafted on other cultures and thrive on them. The products of civilization are devices—things, which can be carried to other places, techniques, which can be learned. Every invention, every process, wherever it may originate, today spreads over the whole world, leaving its cultural foundations behind, and impinges on the lives of people for whom it has no familiar form, no associations, no relations to other products or acts—nothing but usefulness. Finally, civilization as a whole descends like an iron grill to crush the heritage of feeling and faith and the beauty of life.

Civilization—the practical structure of life—is like an outline tracing of the culture that begot it. As long as an outline lies on the painting from which it is made it takes special attention to abstract it; but moved away it appears as a stark and empty form, and imposed on another painting it makes for confusion. Our modern technology, transferred to practically all countries in the world, has caused civilization everywhere to follow its lines, and to change the conduct of life so radically that actuality and tradition seem to have no contact with each other. Even religious practices become untenable in the new practical frame; and with any failure of religious support, individuals tend to lose their emotional and moral stability. The community of feeling disintegrates when institutions lose their sacredness and seem merely old-fashioned, not venerable.

It is easy enough to understand why a civilization engendered by one localized and rather young culture should confuse the rest of the world, but why does it affront and challenge the society that gave it birth? We all feel the same insecurity in the face of our miraculous technological progress, which seems to race faster and faster toward complete control of the waters and fires on earth, the hidden powers of chemicals in the earth, the forces of light, air pressure, and the rotation of the globe itself, and even toward the conquest of interstellar space.

The fact is, I think, that scientific production has outrun our imagination, and the change in our civilization —in the practical means and techniques of life—has advanced with a gathered momentum of its own and outstripped the advance of our thinking. Our technological civilization, consequently, seems to overtake and overwhelm us as though it were something foreign coming in on us; it makes all our traditional institutions seem inadequate, so that we tend to abandon them. State religion, marriage, paternal authority, deference to the aged, piety toward the dead, holiness and rank and royalty —all these ancient values have lost their inviolable status and need to be defended against the iconoclastic "modern spirit." Sometimes, for all the defenses that the older generation can put up for them, a younger generation sweeps them away as relics of a superstitious, slavish, uncivilized past. But with them it sweeps away its own social symbols and the materials of its own world orientation; then personal life suddenly feels empty, and the civilization that shatters its spiritual comforts in the name of practical improvements seems to have come on it like a superimposed power from outside.

This is, I think, an inevitable transition which really marks one of the great crises in human history—the final emergence of world society from the long ages of self-sufficient cultural groups. For science, which is certainly the keynote of our era, is international. It is a human achievement, not a national one. The civilization which is sweeping the whole world, though it is expressed mainly in commerce and new kinds of industry, is a product of science. We are in a socially anomalous state between a world populated by societies with tribal religions and interests, and a world of global industrial organization, populated by a society with global interests but no symbols to express them, no religion to support the individual in this vast new theater of life.

Such disharmonies of growth are well known to every naturalist; and what can happen in biological evolution can happen in psychological and social evolution, too. That strange emergence of new forms which my late friend and revered teacher, Alfred North Whitehead, called "the creative advance of nature," is not an orderly process. It is full of irregularities. According to the fossil record, some animals like the horse which attained great body size came near to extinction before some other trait—the development of the brain, for instance, or of feet to bear the added weight—caught up with the sudden increase. In the development of society there seems to be a similar unevenness, making for excess powers and cultural lags. When such transitional disproportions occur, strains are set up in the social organism which only time can even out. A new culture is probably in the making, which will catch up with the changed human environment that our runaway, freewheeling civilization has visited on us. But one cannot force the emergence of a real culture. It begins when imagination catches fire, and objects and actions become life symbols, and the new life symbols become motifs of art. Art, which formulates and fixes human ways of feeling, is always the spearhead of a new culture, for culture is the objective record of developed feeling.

What really fulfills and establishes a culture, however,

is not art, but something that follows—the deeply and tacitly felt life of overt action, institutions, ways of living, things produced. Philosophy, law, exploration, marital virtues, religion—all have characterized various cultures in the past. We do not know what the driving force and the substance of the next cultural epoch will be, but I suspect that, as so often in nature, the same development which is breaking the old frame of our thinking will fashion the new one: namely, the development of science. My suspicion rests on several facts. One I just mentioned—that, as Pflüger said, "the cause of the need is the cause of the fulfillment of the need." The destructive force which shatters so many old cultures is really constructive of the new; the upheavals in the world are transitional functions. Another is the universal, global character of science. A culture that can embrace a world-wide civilization will probably be a global culture, encompassing all humanity. At present, scientific thinking is the only one of our great and prevailing activities which is universal in fact as well as in principle. We already claim the universality of art, and gradually come to appreciate other people's art, but it still starts by being exotic and often remains so even if we know and love it. Science is not native or exotic; it belongs to humanity and is the same wherever it is found. Only it is not likely to beget a culture unless, and until, a truly universal artistic imagination catches fire from its torch and serves without deliberate intent to give shape to a new feeling, such as generally initiates a new epoch of society. Then the intellectual growth of science will have a vanguard to follow up and a "line of growth" to establish.

This growth is not likely to make recognizable progress in our own days, but that does not mean that no progress is going on. The great movements of society, the characteristic achievements of whole ages, do not gather force and form quickly. A scientific mentality capable of engendering a world culture will have to go far beyond what we call by its name today; it will have to liberate and yet discipline a great imagination, encompass such subjects as mind, growth, language, and history, and produce social concepts that have meaning for a humanity which inhabits the whole earth and reaches for other stars. That is no five-year plan; it is no plan at all, but will happen or not happen without our resolutions to have it thus or otherwise. But something has to happen, of course, to break the tensions that are still building up today. There are signs of it already, and the youngest of us may live to see the beginnings, probably in one or another of the arts, of a new feeling, destined to be the spearhead of a culture which will catch up with our runaway technological civilization, and overcome the outward violence and inward uncertainty which is the price of our first truly international possession—scientific thought.

7 MAN AND ANIMAL: THE CITY AND THE HIVE*

WITHIN THE PAST five or six decades, the human scene has probably changed more radically than ever before in history. The outward changes in our own setting are already an old story: the disappearance of horse-drawn vehicles, riders, children walking to school, and the advent of the long, low, powerful Thing in their stead; the transformation of the mile wide farm into a ticktacktoe of lots, each sprouting a split-level dream home. These are the obvious changes, more apparent in the country than in the city. The great cities have grown greater, brighter, more mechanized, but their basic patterns seem less shaken by the new power and speed in which the long industrial revolution culminates.

The deepest change, however, is really a change in our picture of mankind, and that is most spectacular where mankind is teeming and concentrated—in the city. Our old picture of human life was a picture of local groups, each speaking its mother tongue, observing some established religion, following its own customs. It might be a civilized community or a savage tribe, but it had its distinct traditions. And in it were subdivisions, usually families, with their more special local ties and human relations.

Today, natural tribes and isolated communities have all but disappeared. The ease and speed of travel, the swift economic changes that send people in search of new

* This paper, read at the Cooper Union in New York, was published in *The Antioch Review* (Fall, 1958) and reprinted in *Society Today and Tomorrow*, E. F. Hunt and Jules Karlin, eds. N. Y.: Macmillan, 1961.

kinds of work, the two wars that swept over all boundaries, have wiped out most of our traditions. The old family structure is tottering. Society tends to break up into new and smaller units—in fact, into its ultimate units, the human individuals that compose it.

This atomization of society is most obvious in a great cosmopolitan city. The city seems to be composed of millions of unrelated individuals, each scrambling for himself, yet each caught in the stream of all the others.

Discerning eyes saw this a hundred years ago, especially in industrial cities, where individuals from far or near came to do what other individuals from far or near had also come to do—each a cog in the new machine. Most of the cogs had no other relation to each other. And ever since this shake-up in society began, a new picture of society has been in the making—the picture of *human masses,* brought together by some outside force, some imposed function, into a superpersonal unit—masses of people, each representing an atom of "manpower" in a new sort of organism, the industrial state.

The idea of the state as a higher organism—the state as a superindividual—is old. But our conception of such a state is new, because our industrial civilization, which begets our atomized society, is new. The old picture was not one of masses driven by some imposed economic power, or any other outside power. The superindividual was a rational being, directed by a mind within it. The guardians of the state, the rulers, were its mind. Plato described the state as "the man writ large." Hobbes, two thousand years later, called it "Leviathan," the great creature. A city-state like ancient Athens or Sparta might be "a man writ large," but England was too big for that. It was the big fish in the big pond. The mind of Hobbes's fish was perhaps subhuman, but it was still single and sovereign in the organism.

Another couple of centuries later, Rudyard Kipling, faced with a democratic, industrialized civilization, called his allegory of England, "The Mother Hive." Here, a common will, dictated by complicated instincts, replaced even Leviathan's mind; each individual was kept in line by the blind forces of the collective life.

The image of the hive has had a great success as an

ideal of collaborative social action. Every modern utopia (except the completely wishful Shangri-La) reflects the beehive ideal. Even a statesman of highest caliber, Jan Smuts, has praised it as a pattern for industrial society. Plato's personified state and Hobbes's sea monster impress us as fantasies, but the hive looks like more than a poetic figure; it seems really to buzz around us.

I think the concept of the state as a collective organism, composed of multitudes of little workers, guided by social forces that none of the little workers can fathom, and accomplishing some greater destiny, is supported by a factor other than our mechanized industry; that other factor is a momentous event in our intellectual history: the spread of the theory of evolution.

First biologists, then psychologists, and finally sociologists and moralists have become newly aware that man belongs to the animal kingdom. The impact of the concept of evolution on scientific discovery has been immense, and it has not stopped at laboratory science; it has also produced some less sober and sound inspirations. The concept of continuous animal evolution has made most psychologists belittle the differences between man and his nonhuman relatives, and led some of them, indeed, to think of *Homo sapiens* as just one kind of primate among others, like the others in all essential respects—differing from apes and monkeys not much more than they differ from species to species among themselves. Gradually the notion of the human animal became common currency, questioned only by some religious minds. This in turn has made it natural for social theorists with scientific leanings to model their concepts of human society on animal societies, the anthill and the beehive.

Perhaps it were well, at this point, to say that I myself stand entirely in the scientific camp. I do not argue against any religious or even vitalistic doctrines; such things are not arguable. I speak not *for*, but *from,* a naturalist's point of view, and anyone who does not share it can make his own reservations in judging what I say.

Despite man's zoological status, which I wholeheartedly accept, there is a deep gulf between the highest animal and the most primitive normal human being: a difference in mentality that is fundamental. It stems from the development of one new process in the human brain—a process that seems to be entirely peculiar to that brain: the use of *symbols for ideas.* By "symbols" I mean all kinds of signs that can be used and understood whether the things they refer to are there or not. The word "symbol" has, unfortunately, many different meanings for different people. Some people reserve it for mystic signs, like Rosicrucian symbols; some mean by it *significant images,* such as Keats' "Huge cloudy symbols of a high romance"; some use it quite the opposite way and speak of "mere symbols," meaning empty gestures, signs that have lost their meanings; and some, notably logicians, use the term for mathematical signs, marks that constitute a code, a brief, concise language. In their sense, ordinary words are symbols, too. Ordinary language is a symbolism.

When I say that the distinctive function of the human brain is the use of symbols, I mean any and all of these kinds. They are all different from signs that animals use. Animals interpret signs, too, but only as pointers to actual things and events, cues to action or expectation, threats and promises, landmarks and earmarks in the world. Human beings use such signs, too, but above all they use symbols—especially words—to think and talk about things that are neither present nor expected. The words convey *ideas,* that may or may not have counterparts in actuality. This power of thinking *about* things expresses itself in language, imagination, and speculation—the chief products of human mentality that animals do not share.

Language, the most versatile and indispensable of all symbolisms, has put its stamp on all our mental functions, so that I think they always differ from even their closest analogues in animal life. Language has invaded our feeling and dreaming and action, as well as our reasoning, which is really a product of it. The greatest change wrought by language is the increased scope of awareness in speech-gifted beings. An animal's awareness is always of things in its own place and life. In human awareness, the present, actual situation is often the least part. We have not only memories and expectations; we have *a past* in which we locate our memories, and *a future* that vastly overreaches our own anticipations. Our past is a story, our future a piece of imagination. Likewise our ambient is a place in a wider, symbolically conceived place, the universe. We live in *a world*.

This difference of mentality between man and animal seems to me to make a cleft between them almost as great as the division between animals and plants. There is continuity between the orders, but the division is real nevertheless. Human life differs radically from animal life. By virtue of our incomparably wider awareness, of our power of envisagement of things and events beyond any actual perception, we have acquired needs and aims that animals do not have; and even the most savage human society, having to meet those needs and implement those aims, is not really comparable to any animal society. The two may have some analogous functions, but the essential structure must be different, because man and beast live differently in every way.

Probably the profoundest difference between human and animal needs is made by one piece of human awareness, one fact that is not present to animals, because it is never learned in any direct experience: that is our foreknowledge of death. The fact that we ourselves must die is not a simple and isolated fact. It is built on a wide survey of facts that discloses the structure of history as a succession of overlapping brief lives, the patterns of youth and age, growth and decline; and above all that, it is built on the logical insight that *one's own life is a case in point*. Only a creature that can think symbolically *about* life can conceive of its own death. Our knowledge of death is part of our knowledge of life.

What, then, do we—all of us—know about life?

Every life that we know is generated from other life. Each living thing springs from some other living thing or things. Its birth is a process of new individuation, in a life stream whose beginning we do not know.

Individuation is a word we do not often meet. We hear about individuality, sometimes spoken in praise, sometimes as an excuse for someone's being slightly crazy. We hear and read about "the individual," a being that is forever adjusting, like a problem child, to something called "society." But how does individuality arise? What makes an individual? A fundamental, biological process of *individuation,* that marks the life of every stock, plant or animal. Life is a series of individuations, and these can be of various sorts, and reach various degrees.

Most people would agree, offhand, that every creature lives its life and then dies. This might, indeed, be called a truism. But, like some other truisms, it is not true. The lowest forms of life, such as the amoebae, normally (that is, barring accidents) do not die. When they grow very large and might be expected to lay eggs, or in some other way raise a family, they do no such thing; they divide, and make two small ones ready to grow. Well now, where is the old one? It did not die. But it is gone. Its individuation was only an episode in the life of the stock, a phase, a transient form that changed again. Amoebae are individuated in space—they move and feed as independent, whole organisms—but in time they are not self-identical individuals. They do not generate young ones while they themselves grow old; they grow old and *become* young ones.

All the higher animals, however, are final individuations that end in death. They spring from a common stock, but they do not merge back into it. Each one is an end. Somewhere on its way toward death it usually produces a new life to succeed it, but its own story is finished by death.

That is our pattern, too. Each human individual is a culmination of an inestimably long line—its ancestry— and each is destined to die. The living stock is like a palm tree, a trunk composed of its own past leaves. Each leaf springs from the trunk, unfolds, grows, and dies off; its past is incorporated in the trunk, where new life has usually arisen from it. So there constantly are ends, but the stock lives on, and each leaf has that whole life behind it.

The momentous difference between us and our animal cousins is that they do not know they are going to die. Animals spend their lives avoiding death, until it gets them. They do not know it is going to. Neither do they know that they are part of a greater life, but pass on the torch without knowing. Their aim, then, is simply to keep going, to function, to escape trouble, to live from moment to moment in an endless Now.

Our power of symbolic conception has given us each a glimpse of himself as one final individuation from the great human stock. We do not know when or what the end will be, but we know that there will be one. We also envisage a past and future, a stretch of time so vastly longer than any creature's memory, and a world so much richer than any world of sense, that it makes our time in that world seem infinitesimal. This is the price of the great gift of symbolism.

In the face of such uncomfortable prospects (probably conceived long before the dawn of any religious ideas), human beings have evolved aims different from those of any other creatures. Since we cannot have our fill of existence by going on and on, we want to have *as much life as possible* in our short span. If our individuation must be brief, we want to make it complete; so we are inspired to think, act, dream our desires, create things, express our ideas, and in all sorts of ways make up by concentration what we cannot have by length of days. We seek the greatest possible individuation, or development of personality. In doing this, we have set up a new demand, not for mere continuity of existence, but for *self-realization*. That is a uniquely human aim.

But obviously, the social structure could not arise on this principle alone. Vast numbers of individualists realizing themselves with a vengeance would not make up an ideal society. A small number might try it; there is a place, far away from here, called the Self-Realization Golden World Colony. But most of us have no golden world to colonize. You can only do that south of Los Angeles.

Seriously, however, an ideal is not disposed of by pointing out that it cannot be implemented under existing conditions. It may still be a true ideal; and if it is very important we may have to change the conditions, as we will have to for the ideal of world peace. If complete individuation were really the whole aim of human life, our society would be geared to it much more than it is. It is not the golden world that is wanting, but something else; the complete individualist is notoriously not the happy man, even if good fortune permits his antics.

The fact is that *the greatest possible individuation* is usually taken to mean, "as much as is possible without curtailing the rights of others." But that is not the real measure of how much is possible. The measure is provided in the individual himself, and is as fundamental as his knowledge of death. It is the other part of his insight into nature—his knowledge of life, of the great unbroken stream, the life of the stock from which his individuation stems.

One individual life, however rich, still looks infinitesimal; no matter how much self-realization is concentrated in it, it is a tiny atom—and we don't like to be tiny atoms, not even hydrogen atoms. We need more than fullness of personal life to counter our terrible knowledge of all it implies. And we have more; we have our history, our commitments made for us before we were born, our relatedness to the rest of mankind. The counterpart of individuation from the great life of the stock is our rootedness in that life, our involvement with the whole human race, past and present.

Each person is not only a free, single end, like the green palm leaf that unfolds, grows in a curve of beauty, and dies in its season; he is like the whole palm leaf, the part inside the trunk, too. He is the culmination of his entire ancestry, and *represents* that whole human past. In his brief individuation he is an *expression* of all humanity. That is what makes each person's life sacred and all-important. A single ruined life is the bankruptcy of a long line. This is what I mean by the individual's involvement with all mankind.

All animals are unconsciously involved with their kind. Heredity governs not only their growth, color, and form, but their actions, too. They carry their past about with them in everything they do. But they do not know it. They don't need to, because they never could lose it. Their involvement with the greater life of the race is implicit in their limited selfhood.

Our knowledge that life is finite, and, in fact, precarious and brief, drives us on to greater individuation than animals attain. Our mental talents have largely freed us from that built-in behavior called instinct. The scope of our imagination gives each of us a separate world, and a separate consciousness, and threatens to break the instinctual ties of brotherhood that make all the herrings swim into one net, and all the geese turn their heads at the same moment. Yet we cannot afford to lose the feeling of involvement with our kind; for if we do, personal life shrinks up to nothingness.

The sense of involvement is our social sense. We have it by nature, originally just as animals do, and just as unconsciously. It is the direct feeling of needing our own kind, caring what happens. Social sense is an instinctive sense of being somehow one with all other people—a feeling that reflects the rootedness of our existence in a human past. Human society rests on this feeling. It is often said to rest on the need of collaboration, or on domination of the weak by the strong, or some other circumstance, but I think such theories deal with its modes, and ignore its deeper structure; at the bottom of it is the feeling of involvement, or social sense. If we lose that, no coercion will hold us to our duties, because they do not feel like commitments, and no achievements will matter, because they are doomed to be snuffed out with the individual, without being laid to account in the continuity of life.

Great individual development, such as human beings are driven by their intellectual insights to seek, does of course always threaten to break the bonds of direct social involvement, that give animal life its happy unconscious continuity. When the strain gets hard, we have social turmoil, anarchy, irresponsibility, and in private lives the sense of loneliness and infinite smallness that lands some people in nihilism and cynicism, and leads others to existentialism or less intellectual cults.

It is then that social philosophers look on animal societies as models for human society. There is no revolt, no strike, no competition, no anti-Anything party, in a beehive. As Kipling, fifty years or more ago, represented his British utopia, which he called the Mother Hive, that ideal state had a completely co-operative economy, an army that went into action without a murmur, each man with the same impulse the moment an enemy threatened to intrude, and a populace of such tribal solidarity that it would promptly run out any stranger that tried to become established in the state and disrupt its traditions. Any native individual that could not fit into the whole had to be liquidated; the loss was regrettable, but couldn't be helped, and would be made up.

Yet the beehive really has no possible bearing on human affairs, for it owes its harmonious existence to the fact that its members are *incompletely individuated,* even as animals go. None of them performs all of a creature's essential functions: feeding, food getting, nest building, mating, and procreating. The queen has to be fed and tended; she has only procreative functions. She doesn't even bring up her own children; they have nurses. The drones are born and reared only as her suitors, and when the romance is finished they are killed, like proper romantic heroes. The building, nursing, food getting, and fighting are done by sterile females who cannot procreate, amazons who do all their own housework. So there is not only division of labor, but division of organs, functional and physical incompleteness. This direct involvement of each bee with the whole lets the hive function with an organic rhythm that makes its members appear wonderfully socialized. But they are really not socialized at all, any more than the cells in our tissues are socialized; they are associated, by being unindividuated.

That is as far away from a human ideal as one can get. We need, above all, a world in which we can realize our capacities, develop and act as personalities. That means giving up our instinctive patterns of habit and prejudice, our herd instincts. Yet we need the emotional security of the greater, continuous life—the awareness of our involvement with all mankind. How can we eat that cake, and have it too?

The same mental talent that makes us need so much individuation comes to the rescue of our social involvement: I mean the peculiarly human talent of holding ideas in the mind by means of symbols. Human life, even in the simplest forms we know, is shot through and through with *social symbols.* All fantastic beliefs in a great ancestor are symbolic of the original and permanent life of the stock from which every individual life stems. The totem, the hero, the sacred cow, these are the most elementary social symbols. With a maturer view of the world, and the development of religious ideas, the symbolic image of man is usually taken up into the greater view of a divine world order and a moral law. We are sons of Adam and daughters of Eve. If Adam and Eve were simply some human couple supposed to have lived in the Near East before it was so difficult, this would be an odd way of speaking; we don't ordinarily refer to our neighbor's children as Mr. Brown's boys and Mrs. Brown's girls. But Adam is Man, and Eve is Woman (the names even mean that): and among us transient little mites, every man is Man, every woman is Woman. That is the source of human dignity, the sense of which has to be upheld at all levels of social life.

Most people have some religious ritual that supports their knowledge of a greater life, but even in purely secular affairs we constantly express our faith in the continuity of human existence. Animals provide lairs or nests for their immediate offspring. Man builds for the future —often for nothing else. His earliest great buildings were not mansions, but monuments. And not only physical edifices, but above all laws and institutions are intended for the future, and often justified by showing that they have a precedent, or are in accord with the past. They are conveniences of their day, but symbols of more than their day. They are symbols of society, and of each individual's inalienable membership in society.

What, then, is the measure of our possible individuation, without loss of social sense? It is the power of social symbolism. We can give up our actual, instinctual involvements with our kind just to the extent that we can replace them by symbolic ones. This is the prime function of social symbols, from a handshake, to the assembly of robed judges in a Supreme Court. In protocol and ritual, in the investment of authority, in sanctions and honors, lies our security against loss of involvement with mankind; in such bonds lies our freedom to be individuals.

It has been said that an animal society, like a beehive, is really an organism, and the separate bees its organic parts. I think this statement requires many reservations, but it contains some truth. The hive is an organic structure, a superindividual, something like an organism. A human city, however, is an *organization*. It is above all a symbolic structure, a mental reality. Its citizens are the whole and only individuals. They are not a "living mass," like a swarm of semi-individuated bees. The model of the hive has brought with it the concept of human masses, to be cared for in times of peace, deployed in times of war, educated for use or sacrificed for the higher good of their state. In the specious analogy of animal and human society, the hive and the city, lies, I think, the basic philosophical fallacy of all totalitarian theory, even the most sincere and idealistic—even the thoroughly noble political thought of Plato.

We are like leaves of the palm tree, each deeply embedded in the tree, a part of the trunk, each opening to the light in a final, separate life. Our world is a human world, organized to implement our highest individuation. There may be ten thousand of us working in one factory. There are several millions of us living in a city like New York. But we are not the masses; we are the public.

8 THE ULTIMATE UNIT*

SINCE YOU have done me the honor of inviting me to speak at an essentially sociological conference, although I am not a social scientist but a student of philosophy, I assume that you wish to pause in the fact finding and planning which are our main purpose here, to reflect philosophically on the facts and acts under discussion.

To reflect philosophically is to reflect on the meanings of our own words, and on the implications of the statements we are entertaining. When the terms of a serious discourse are very exactly scrutinized—which is the first business of philosophy—many such terms which seemed to have quite clear and definite meanings prove to be vague and hard to define. They often have an emotional aura that makes the discourse persuasive; Professor Lovejoy has called this their good or bad "metaphysical pathos." But what should make one suspect that they are vague is, above all, that our most earnest thoughts lodged in those terms do not have immediate implications which lead to all sorts of specific elaborations and unexpected insights.

The key words in the topics proposed for our present discussion are *individual, society, creative experience, science,* and *art.* Obviously we cannot examine them all; but the very first one—*individual*—is perhaps the most important, and happens to be the one which I find the most problematical as a working concept.

The word "individual" has meant many things in many

* This paper was read at The International Conference held at the Vassar College Centenary, March, 1961.

contexts and even in a single one. In biology it generally means a creature that can carry on the basic life functions apart from others, though it may prefer to be in company. Almost at once we are faced with certain anomalies. Is a hydra an individual? It and several companions have a common stomach and vascular system. Is the male of the marine worm *Bonnelia viridis* an individual? It is tiny, parasitic on the female, and spends its adult life in her uterus; yet in infancy it is independent, and unless it happens to sit down on the proboscis of a female (which the young like to do), it will become a female itself. There are many other pseudo- or semi-individuals. In speaking of human beings we often use the word "individual" in a laudatory sense: a true individual is morally responsible, serious, brave, and—oddly enough —more interested in others than in himself, and so on. But when we speak of "*the* individual and society," we mean the average person, who has precious few such virtues. We slide from one concept to another, if you will even call such vague meanings concepts—for who has ever defined "the average person"?

The term "individual" is very hard to define in a usable way, for the definition should be widely and yet precisely variable to fit many sorts of individuals, from the problematical semi-individuals to Leviathan and Superman, from flowers in the crannied wall to poets who pluck them. But a noun with adjectives to characterize the varieties of things it covers expresses no working concept that relates the varieties and directs one to possible further ones. It is often more enlightening to work with terms that designate the *process* which engenders the thing in question and produces its various forms under different conditions.

The process that gives rise to individuals is immensely complex, but may be broadly designated as *individuation*. Despite the complexity of all its manifestations, it embodies a fundamental biological principle that operates in countless different circumstances, each of which makes the product, the individual, special if not unique. I find the concept of individuation much more useful than that of individuality, for reasons that I think every scientist can guess at once: a process has degrees and directions.

A creature may be highly individuated in one direction and very little in another. For instance, robins are more closely involved with their parents in infancy—that is, less quickly individuated—than geese; geese feed themselves and move under their own steam as soon as they are hatched, while baby robins acquire such individual powers only gradually. But in another way robins are more individuated than geese; as adults, they act separately in response to the environment, whereas geese act in chorus. If one goose gets up, they all do; if one sits down they all sit down. There is no single factor of individuality present in different quantities in robins and geese, respectively. There are different forms of individuation: physical—as in the case of a mutant in a hereditary line, or, to stay nearer home, of a person who looks like nobody else in the family—vital, like the cat who walks by himself—or mental. This last form is incomparably greater in human beings than in all other creatures, but varies widely even among us. So do all the other forms.

Another advantage of starting with the concept of individuation is that there is a converse process, which tends to hold a balance against it: the converse of individuation is *involvement*. I find that some very baffling problems about the relations of individuals to society become negotiable if they are treated in terms of individuation and involvement and the effects of any sudden or far-reaching change in the balance of those two biological principles.

It is customary, in talking about society, to begin with an idea of a particular society, usually a somewhat schematized imaginary tribe living in an unspecified wilderness and doing nothing but hunting big game, fighting exactly similar rival tribes, and dancing in triumph. The relation of a generalized member called "the individual" to this tribe is taken as the typical case, of which all actually known relations of members to social groups are variants.

That, however, is starting on a level that is already cultural, and for scientific purposes has the drawback of being fictitious. I find it better to take the running start for my speculative leap farther back, and on somewhat harder ground. Let me say a few words about the pattern of individuation, and especially its limit, species involvement, in a more general frame of animal existence.

Among such very primitive creatures as I have already mentioned, physical individuation may be visibly incomplete. Among some higher ones, for instance bees and ants, apparently complete individuals may not have the full complement of organs that would make them viable in isolation. Even in mammals—including man—one form of species involvement remains essential: they cannot procreate without conjoint action. The offspring are physically made from parts of two parents. In most of the species, moreover, each birth is followed by a period during which the new life is dependent on one or both parents for its nurture. During this time its elementary behavioral patterns mature, the individual life unfolds.

That is what primarily I mean by saying each living creature is rooted in the life of an indefinitely long-lived stock and achieves a certain degree of individuation, typical of its kind, and variously furthered or fettered by its chance conditions. Not only its bodily structure, but its impulses and the structure of its acts are inherited patterns. Animals are bound to repeat the repertoire of their ancestors because they are continuations of one long-evolved process. A cat is committed to feline activities, roving and essentially self-reliant, as a gopher is committed to his group life and his intense domesticity.

In the solitary animals (solitary except for episodes of mating and puerperium), individual existence has to be maintained by constant defense, escape, self-assertion, often in competition with other individuals of the same sort. In herd or hive animals certain influences that establish familiarity reduce this self-maintaining action within the group; but groups usually take a hostile attitude toward each other and toward members of other groups as parts of hostile colonies. That is to say, the phyletic stock is broken up into separate self-continuing *stocks*. The principle of individuation operates to make larger, continuing units, often with smaller subdivisions, of which the mortal individual is the final subunit.

Since we are concerned just now with human mortal individuals let us turn to the human stock and its peculiarities, which have carried its individuating processes beyond those of any other species. Before the dawn of any cultural phenomena—before speech, dance, custom, or moral obligation—our ancestry was one of the primate stocks. Comparative anatomy puts that beyond question. But it must have been marked by some traits that were not found in the species which were most analogous to it, the precursors of our great apes. Above all, a highly developed brain was very probably a specialty of the Hominidae. Such a trait is apt to give a radical turn to the further development of a species.

We do not know whether our kind in its purely animal stages lived in droves or in single families, pairing permanently as some forest animals do or mating promiscuously; but at times there must have been gathered hordes, because in scattered lives the all-important humanizing habit could probably not have taken root—the habit of speech. This activity springs more from the over grown brain than from the creature's other anatomical specialties, though ear, larynx, and delicately mobile mouth parts are necessary for it. The origin of speech is entirely unknown, but whatever guess we make at it rests on complex conditions which must have come together in this particular primate stock. We cannot enter into these questions here, except to note that the deepest and most momentous specialization, the thing that started humanity on its career as something more than an animal species, was the development of symbolic expression and symbolic understanding. Language has given us a means of communication with each other, but above all the power of thought, the awareness of many things at once which are not all given together in experience, and the power of conceiving things and conditions which do not exist at all. Our lives are always lived in a frame of possibility and conceptual assumptions which animals cannot share. They live in an environment variously felt; man lives in a world, which stays there when he sleeps or dreams or gives himself over to his fictitious conceptions.

The power of symbolism creates the need of symbols. We *need* to live in the conceptual frame of a world much larger than the environment we sensuously perceive, or realize from moment to moment in actual expectation, as animals do. We are partially freed from the operations of instinct, which are touched off by environmental factors, because we act in a world of thought. The smallness or greatness of a creature's ambient is the measure of its individual freedom, that is, the directions and the extent to which its individuation can go. In accordance with our mentally widened and mentally structured world, it is our mental life that has the greatest scope for individuation. The human individual is essentially a mental being.

To a creature with a need for symbolic expression and a constant tendency to find symbolic values, nature furnishes symbols of everything emotionally important. The naturally engendered and isolated tribe, be it large or small, which corresponds to the separate hive or pack of animals maintaining its integrity even against its own kind, for man becomes the symbol of something he could not otherwise grasp—humanity. Many tribes call themselves by a name that means "man." Yet they cannot consciously imagine mankind as such. This symbolic function of the tribe is unconsciously accepted. Our unconsciously accepted symbols are the most powerful; in conscious experience they figure not as symbols, but as sacred things. Often the tribe itself is symbolically represented by a totem, a divine dynasty, a patron god, or even the god's name, which is invested with the character of holiness. Humanity is too vast to be directly conceived; it has to be symbolized. But it is this symbolic value that makes the natural unit a social unit, for humanity is more than a species—it is society, and its continuity is history. The actively recognized involvement of each person with the social unit to which he belongs attests and upholds his involvement with his kind, expressed particularly by the commitments which are made for him by his birth into that unit—be it a tribe, a clan, a class, or any other hereditary frame.

I said before, though only in passing, that symbolic conception freed us from the operation of instinct. An animal's instinctive activity is its lifelong, actual, and ineluctable involvement in the way of its kind, its participation in the life of the stock. If its instincts failed or wavered it would be undone, for it has no other mechanism for initiating any action. A robin without its nest-building instinct would not know what to do about its eggs; it might even be unable to produce them. Nothing serves better to show the reciprocal relation between the principles of individuation and involvement than animal instinct. Animals act by instinct—a lifelong commitment to the ways of their kind—to preserve themselves as individuals. The particular life form of the stock is at once the limit and the guarantee of their separate existence.

In man, the animal instincts are too much reduced to be reliable starters or guides of group action or personal behavior. What has suppressed them and gradually displaced them is the high activity of the brain, the special ability to operate with symbols which is manifested in conception, speech, and speculative thought on all levels, from simple, practical cause-and-effect reasoning to the most difficult abstract theories.

Is man, then, exempt from the need of involvement with his own kind? Is he physically, practically, and emotionally self-sufficient? Physically, no more than other mammals. His beginning is in sexual union, his infancy long and completely dependent. Practically, he can do fairly well as Robinson Crusoe—but so can most animals. Emotionally he is certainly not self-sufficient. Loneliness is one of his hazards. But, as a great biologist has said, in nature "the source of the need is the source of the fulfillment of the need." [1] The mental function of symbolization, which augments the scope of our world so that no system of instinctive responses could meet its demands, and therefore breaks the most constant bond of the individual to its kind, makes this bond largely unnecessary to us by providing symbols of our participation in the greater life of mankind, symbols of humanity and of our involvement in it. We can push our individuation beyond the limits to which any other creature's can go, without losing the balance between individuation and involvement, because we have symbolic substitutes for the natural bonds which we give up. And I think it may be generally said that we can afford to become individualized just to the extent that we can replace the natural ties

[1] E. F. W. Pflüger.

which used to hold us to our kind by symbolic ones: obligations, recognition of hereditary commitments, pieties, sanctions, honors, and above all the diverse rites of holy communion.

It may seem odd at this point—more than halfway through the lecture—to say that everything I have said so far is by way of introduction, but so it is. One trouble with philosophizing is that before you reach any interesting implications you have to analyze so many lumpy ideas. Perhaps we had better take inventory of the notions I have tried to clarify so far, because they are needed before I can present you with the view of the human individual's position in society today, to which I hope you will give consideration before this conference is over.

An *individual* is hard to define, since there are partially or vaguely individual beings; and even among unmistakably individual creatures, their individuality rests on different, sometimes incommensurable traits.

It is more profitable to study the processes of *individuation,* which are quite various, take different directions, go on at different rates of speed, and attain different degrees.

Individuation is one of the basic and ubiquitous biological principles, manifested in all of animate nature, and taking the most diverse forms.

One scientific advantage of the concept of individuation is that its negative is not just the privative concept of nonindividuation, but an important condition, sometimes even a reverse process: the *involvement* of a creature with the living stock from which its individuation springs.

The *stock* is the original living entity of indefinite duration. No individual creature can originate or survive without being to some degree involved with the parent stock.

Involvement can take many forms. Procreation, and in higher forms of life the sexual union preceding procreation, constitute the most elementary, physical rootedness of each individual in the continuum of life here called the stock. Repetition of basic forms known as *inheritance* is another bond. It may be bodily form or behavioral. Animals run true to type even in elaborate behavior, the *instinctual* pattern.

Man differs from all other creatures in the form and function of his brain. The cerebral function which sets him apart more than anything else is his use of symbols to formulate and hold ideas. Symbolic activity begets language, religion, art, logical insight, and the power of carrying on a train of abstract thoughts, or reasoning. All imagination requires symbols. All conception is symbolic.

Animals depend on their instincts for self-preservation. Man cannot rely on any built-in behavior patterns. The range of his possible actions has been so enormously widened by his conceptual powers—imagination, cognition, and speculation—that no inherited repertoire could fit the contingencies of his world.

But the natural ties to his kind which he loses with the great growth of his mind are replaced by that same mental power which broke them, the power of symbolization; and we can afford to carry our individuation just as far as symbols of our social involvement hold the balance against it.

So now, after all these preliminaries, we come close to the problem I am setting out so circuitously to discuss— the problem which bears directly on topics of our present meetings. What has happened to the relations of individuals to society that makes us aware of them as never before, and makes us feel vaguely if not acutely that something is wrong between them?

Again I must ask you to look at one of the most general patterns in nature, the evolution of higher forms from primitive ones in vital activity. The lowest organisms have no special organs. They react as a whole to light, temperature, and even food. Any part of an amoeba can momentarily become anything, make any response in the creature's repertoire. In higher stages of life, special organs react selectively to the different kinds of stimuli. Still further up the evolutionary ladder we find these organs highly elaborated into complexes of subordinate parts. For instance, the organ of hearing begins as a mechanism for picking up massive vibrations passing through water, earth, or air. Gradually it becomes specialized for sound waves in the air. The inner ear is elaborated so that different frequencies of these waves register as different tones in our hearing, and we have a gamut of distinguishable pitches. The breaking up of the nervous mechanism into special subunits goes on until its function becomes too complicated to be practicable. As long as the vibrations come at rates of hundreds per second, and even up to a couple of thousands, the ear can react differently to slightly different numbers. If we take the sound of 440 v.p.s. as the orchestra's "A," 436 or 444 will sound "out of tune." The ear distinguishes such differences; but when the frequency goes up into the thousands it can no longer perceive differences of 4 v.p.s. Then a major shift takes place; the perceptible differences are no longer gradations on a unit scale, but jump by thousands. This is a shift to a new principle of operation, a redeployment of the subunits, a simplification of the process at a new level of response. It is like a gearshift.

I have burdened you with this rather technical example because it illustrates as clearly as possible what I think is a universal principle of evolution: the differentiation of forms to the smallest functional subunits, and after that a *shift of functions* to entirely new, unpredictably different, big subunits, made out of the smallest ones by a new process which starts here—*integration*. A reversal of the progressive individuation takes place. Old processes give way to new modes of operation proper to the newly integrated organic structures.

This principle of shift of functions may be seen in the development not only of the ear, but also of the eye, or in the motor patterns of some lower animals that have larval phases, and above all in the evolution of the brain as we trace it from the higher animals—say, dogs —to man, where the sensory functions especially have been reallocated, shifted from inner brain centers to the gray matter, the cortex. A man deprived of the part of the cortex used for hearing is deaf; a dog is not—not quite—he still has some primitive hearing in the brain stem. The functional shift in the dog is not complete. In man, it is.

Now let me draw the moral of all these stories. The

same pattern found in organic evolution, that is, in the development of individual beings, obtains in the development of the living stock as one indefinitely long life. We may as well come right to the human stock. We find progressive differentiation, breaking up into subunits, various races of man—a breaking up that we usually cannot trace, but reconstruct after the fact—then further divisions into smaller subunits effected mainly by circumstances which isolate or assemble hereditary lines, forming natural groups—tribes, families—sometimes confluent lines, equally natural expanded groups, such as clans and peoples, and nations. The constitutive units in such groups usually keep some of their identity, as the twelve tribes of Israel and the various familial stocks of the vikings did for a long time. On such historic foundations, dynasties, classes, castes, and other social divisions are based.

Human groups uphold their singleness, their individuation, more fiercely than groups of any other species, because they not only feel but conceive their identity. Among animals, fighting is an episode started by the chance meeting of packs; in human life warfare is an institution, recognized and prepared in times of peace. Its various actions are parceled out among appointed subgroups which may be committees of one: chiefs with their men, councils of chiefs, high commands. Human groups are organized, articulated subunits of the human stock. Not only in self-assertion—hostility toward rivals —but in the whole round of life they have internal structure as well as external boundaries. They are not mere flocks, but societies.

A society is easier to apprehend than the entire human stock ranging back to immemorial time. A tribe has a remembered ancestry, a living membership, a future foreshadowed in the growing children. For such symbol-mongers as human beings are, everything that has any permanent identity tends to acquire symbolic value and be used to embody a greater conception—that is, to mean more than meets the eye. Primitive symbols are made spontaneously out of the forms which nature provides, including forms of behavior; and the social subunit—the tribe, the clan, the church, or the caste with which a person most ardently identifies himself—is his symbol of the greater life which enfolds him, all humanity. He does not know this; in his consciousness the group is all that claims him. But the fact is that he can shift his explicit allegiance from one body to another—from his tribe to his race, or to a mystic brotherhood, or even his family—and somehow the sense of it is always the same, a greater life. The symbolic office of the greater body to which he gives himself is manifested only in his emotion toward it, which would be inexplicable if that body were a purely practical arrangement to implement common affairs.

In the long history that lies equally behind each one of us, the most persistent and active individuating tendencies have been manifested in the evolution of the brain. In place of instinctual behavior, men have developed a form of behavior that derives largely from imagination, cogitation, and judgment, with a conscious moment of *intention* before the body goes into action. This is moral freedom—freedom from the narrow confines of animal reactions in which there are only small options and immediate decisions, no resolutions, policies, or obligations. We are still carrying on our personal individuation. There is a great deal we might say about that, but no time to say it. The fact here in point is that throughout the long ages in which human freedom was evolved, men have held to their symbols of that essential and good human bondage that keeps the tiny death-bound life a part of the greater life of our kind. There seems to be, normally, a long "organismic" or organismlike phase of society in which special offices, functions, and stations become articulated and established by more or less natural processes: "elders" governing the community, or families achieving ascendancy and handing it on by inheritance, men credited with mystical powers founding a priesthood and making some provision for its continuity which becomes automatic. These forms evolve somewhat as tissues in a developing organism become specialized by their position, external exposure, or proximity to sources of general nutrition, so that they form special organs through their particular involvement with the whole. In human society the fighting power is naturally vested in the men from youth to middle life, in whom aggressive impulses, competition, pride, and exuberance combine to make a warrior caste without any conscious design.

Every high culture seems to have gone through such an evolution. Its height is a dynastic absolute monarchy correlated with a strong priesthood, sometimes meeting in the royal personage itself. This structure may be maintained for a long time, because it serves to symbolize the organic unity of human life on a large scale, and permits the long slow process of mental individuation for which we need the assuring symbol of our security in a greater living whole. The emotional expression of that assurance —devoutness and loyalty—is apt to be most complete and ardent in the monarchical, perhaps theocratic phase of national life.

After that, the operation of the individuating principle in the greater whole, the society, begins to outrun the tempo of man's symbol-making capacity; the breaking up of the royal and ecclesiastic order by more and more autonomy of its inherent parts produces legislative and military councils, separate religious bodies, economic power groups not allied with any high and venerated authority. The emotional effect on people as individuals is that the holiness goes out of all institutions. For a great many persons today, some small sectarian church of their own choosing and the family based on holy matrimony are the only things still regarded as sacred. But even they are precarious. The fact is that adherence to a faith is no longer mandatory, and although marriage is still supposed to be lifelong, divorce is generally tolerated. Only a generation or two ago, a divorced person was considered a disgrace to his family, and children of broken homes bore a stigma, though not quite so much as the poor waifs born out of wedlock. Today they are humanely accepted even in so-called "good society." In fact—this is the important upshot of it all—in the more advanced parts of the "western" culture which derives from Europe, *we no longer visit the sins of the fathers on the children.* Please do not conclude that I think we should still do so; I am sure we should not. But that does not mean that people never should have done so, or that nothing is lost by the change.

I think what has happened to society, and is still happening, is that the individuation of its parts has all but reached its limit. Society is breaking up into its ultimate units—single individuals, persons. Many things could be adduced in evidence of this momentous fact if we only had the time. But the fact is that in our western culture, which is, unfortunately, the only one I know, each individual really stands alone, without support of status, or even family background. The recognition of such personal singleness is expressed in the basic principle of democratic government—"each counts for one and only one." Our magistrates are charged to mete out justice "without respect for persons" (meaning *personae,* personages). It is "man for himself" in our world.

I think we are witnessing the beginning of a vast change in society, nothing less than a biological shift of functions to new structures. The organismlike phase of society, in which more and more subordinate forms become articulated, is reaching its close; the new structures which are already in the making—and, indeed, have long been so— are products of *integration,* new wholes made out of very small ones, even out of the ultimate units. In society, such integral forms are *institutions.* In the past, institutions were based on the natural social articulations, and were essentially recognized and sanctioned natural products. In the future they will have to spring more and more from the higher mental processes which are peculiar to man—conscious planning and ruling.

Meanwhile, we are caught in the turbulence of the shift. With the fast breakup of natural social units, our inherited symbols of humanity are failing, and countless people to whom this is happening feel, but cannot understand, their loss of the sense of involvement, which makes the world seem like a meaningless rat race in which they are reduced to nothingness, alone in life and in death. They turn desperately back to religions they had let go or to exotic cults that promise a new mode of salvation, condemn their actual world as false, reject what seems to hurry the fragmentation of society—science, technology, and the cultivation of reason that begot those advances—

and long to return to the unconscious, instinct-guided self-realization of animals, or at least to the tribal pieties they attribute to unknown savages. Meanwhile they do not know that the most dramatic rejection of social involvement lies in their repudiation of the onerous things civilized life visits on them, for our strongest bond to our kind is the acceptance of commitments we did not make, commitments made for us by the circumstances of our birth or the decrees of our elders. No matter how much we want to stop the progress of individuation, our own acts hurry it. Most people today, and especially the thoughtful and serious ones, feel that they are not bound by any commitment they have not made themselves. The most spectacular version of this doctrine is that new governments superseding old, traditional, obsolete ones may repudiate obligations and agreements entered into by their predecessors.

The loss of emotional security with the shattering of our natural symbols—hurried by the two wars which have uprooted millions of people—is patent. And any reintegration of life on new lines—so new that no one can even hazard a guess at its design—is in its infancy; and it will be long before it provides forms which can take on deep social significance and become our symbols of humanity and its place in nature. I have no solution to propose, but have only offered these reflections in the hope of explaining some of the vast ructions that are going on. But one suggestion (for another time, not today) does occur to me. Western culture, essentially European, is relatively young. There are older and maturer cultures in the world, and there are at least a few people here who know them by inheritance and study. I am not referring here to the famous practice of mystical contemplation as a safeguard against excessive individuation, but to a much more mundane matter—the fact that many of those older societies have evolved attitudes toward sex, divorce, and social obligation which may be something we are now approaching. Perchance their own history may have gone through the phase on which ours is just entering; and it is possible that, intentionally or even unwittingly, they may show us some proven ways of keeping our individual lives anchored in the life of humanity, through the maelstrom moment as the evolutionary tide is turning.

9 THE GROWING CENTER OF KNOWLEDGE*

KNOWLEDGE GROWS with exploration, adding new facts, correcting old beliefs. It grows like a tree, at every tip, so that the crown seems to spread out an ever-growing fringe.

A human being is not a tree; our growth is more complicated. We have more than vegetative functions, and therefore more than a vegetative form of growth. But the analogy between physical growth and cultural growth, organic life and mental life, really goes much further than the picturesque figure of the "growing edge of knowledge." The constant multiplication of facts, often effected by breaking up big observations into more exact, measured data which lead in their turn to general but precise information, is the spectacular process in our scientific expansion. It takes place chiefly at the points of newest interest, and this growth of our store of knowledge is like the physical growth of new tissue by proliferation of the cells that compose it.

But in the higher organisms, such as human beings, the whole process of development—the whole *life*—is controlled by a complex organ whose parts pervade most of the body. This is known as the *central nervous system.* It comprises the brain, the spinal cord, and all the nerves; the special organs of sight and hearing, though not made entirely of nervous tissue, are extensions of the brain.

The central nervous system does not increase by multiplying its cells. From infancy to old age we have essen-

* Reprinted from *Frontiers of Knowledge*, ed. by Lynn White, N. Y.: Harper's, 1956.

tially the same nerve cells we started with at birth. (There are a few nerves, for instance in the face, that repair their tissue, but in general destroyed nerve cells can never be replaced.) The nervous system has no "growing edge."

Yet obviously the nervous system of a man is bigger than that of a baby. It has grown somehow. The brain is bigger, though proportionately not much, and the spinal cord is longer. The nerves that reach the man's fingers have farther to go than they used to. In the controlling central organ there is a different kind of increase —not by addition of new cells at the nerve ends or on the surface of the brain, but by growth of the original cells themselves. They stretch. They stretch to keep pace with the growing society of the cells that divide and multiply, and that extend the compass of the body as a growing population extends the compass of a city, suburb by suburb. The nervous system is a *growing center,* that holds all the advancing other parts in mutual alliance as one organism, living one life.

In the cultural life of our day—one of the very surprising days in man's history—the most breathtaking events arise from the sudden increase of scientific knowledge. One discovery leads to another. Every new fact suggests others to be established. When whole series of demonstrable facts fall into line, they exemplify *natural laws,* which are simply the most general facts we know about the universe. Then the "growing edge" ceases to be a fringe of more or less random facts and solidifies into a new part of the body of knowledge.

But in the growth of culture, as in the growth of a high organism, there is something that does not increase by addition of elements, but by modification and stretching that is mentality itself, which comprises much more than knowledge. Pure factual knowledge, however wide, would not constitute a mental life.

Neither a single mind nor the collective mind of a society is solely or even primarily "a blank tablet on which experience writes" its record of ready-made facts. Knowledge of facts is a requisite for the activity of a living brain with all its involvements. The greater, older mental functions are feeling and imagination. Not that these several factors are really separate, or even separable; they are at best *distinguishable*, in a normal mind. If they fall apart, or if one interferes with the natural development of another, there is mental disturbance, which may range from a brief moment of disorientation to the gravest, lifelong imbalance.

Imagination is probably the greatest force acting on our feelings—greater and steadier than outside influences, like fear-inspiring noises and sights (lightning and thunder, an oncoming truck, a raging tiger) or direct sense pleasure, even including the intense pleasures of sexual excitement. Only a small part of reality, for a human being, is what actually is going on; the greater part is what he imagines in connection with the sights and sounds of the moment.

Imagination makes his world. This is not to say that his world is a fantasy, his life a dream, or any such poetic pseudophilosophical thing. It means that his "world" is bigger than the stimuli which surround him, and the measure of it is the reach of his coherent and steady imagination. An animal's environment consists of the things that act on his senses. Absent things which he desires or fears probably have no proxies in his consciousness, like their *images* in ours, but appear, when finally they do, as satisfactions of his driving needs, or crises in his more or less constant watching and reacting. He does not live in a world of unbroken space and time, filled with events even when he is not present or when he is not interested; his "world" has a fragmentary, intermittent existence, arising and collapsing with his activities. A human being's world hangs together, its events fit into each other; no matter how devious their connections, there always are connections, in one big framework of space and time. (The modern concept of "space-time" is a refinement of thought that we shall consider later.) An animal's environment is not really a "world," let alone "*the* world"; his environment is a momentary reality, part of his own activity, influenced by previous experiences but not in ways that bring them back as a "past," and directed toward future experiences but not toward a "future." Past and future, events and states, perhaps even things in their relations to each other, have no part in his perception. *The world* is something human.

What makes the difference is the peculiar tendency of the human brain to use the sense impressions it receives not only as stimuli or obstacles to physical action, but as material for its specialized function, imagination. We not only see things, but at the same time imagine them to have all sorts of properties that one cannot see. Animals respond to outside stimuli either overtly or not at all; but men respond largely in a cerebral, invisible way, producing images, notions, figments of all sorts that serve as *symbols for ideas.* The result is that we live in a web of ideas, a fabric of our own making wherein we catch the contributions of outside reality, sights, sounds, smells, and so on. Actual perceptions come and go, and are beyond our control (except in so far as we may open or shut our eyes, touch things or not, and cause a few changes to happen), but symbols may be found or produced at will, and manipulated with great freedom; by means of them we supplement our fragmentary sensations and build up around each perceptual core a structure of ideas. That is the sense of saying we have ideas *about* what we actually see.

The symbolic rendering of experience is a vast topic that we cannot possibly enter on here. A good deal has been and is still being written about it, for the importance of symbolization is a recent discovery. Suffice it, then, to touch the high points of that all-important process. Its most spectacular product is the great systematic symbolism known as *language,* which engenders the whole mental development that sets men apart from their zoological brethren. The line between animals and men is, I think, precisely the language line. (Animals probably communicate only intentions and direct emotional excitements, not ideas *about* things.) Language serves far greater purposes than even the most elaborate system of signals whereby we might make our wishes known and control each other's behavior. Its first and most astounding function is to shape the human world.

Sense perceptions are only part of the world. They are indispensable elements, but by no means its whole substance. The world for human beings is made up of *facts;* and facts are as much a product of conception as of perception. Facts are "about" things, as our immediate knowledge is "about" our sensory experiences. Our world is not a random collection of things, but a great nexus of physical facts, historical facts, legal and political facts, and especially, for each person, the ever-approaching phalanx of practical facts that he has to meet from hour to hour. What we call "the world" is a conceptual structure of space and time in which events occur, and develop into situations from which new, more or less spectacular events arise; this development is the order of cause and effect as we conceive it, and what develops is reality, the web of facts.

Reality contains all the deliverances of our senses, but its framework is not something visible, tangible, or in any sensuous way perceptible. Its framework is something intellectual, perceptible only through *symbols*. To say it is intellectual is not to say it is reserved for an intelligentsia, or even for civilized races; a common intellectuality belongs to all human beings that are not mentally defective, and impresses itself on their experience at the elementary level of understanding words.

It is sometimes said that words stand proxy for things and acts, and that consequently a dog to whom a word means an object, a person, or an act to be performed understands language. But that is a slipshod argument and false conclusion. The words that a dog "understands" are functioning as signals, like dinner bells and automobile horns. They tell him *of* the things they designate, but not *about* them. They may make him expect his dinner but they cannot inform him that it will be late, or that yesterday's dinner was good. The human use of language, by contrast, is essentially to express ideas about the things mentioned—to call attention to their relations, parts, properties, aspects, and functions, and to the intricate relations of those constituents and functions to each other.

Relations are known to us primarily through words, our most ready and powerful symbols. Though we implicitly take account of relations in action, explicitly they cannot be singled out and pointed to like physical things.

Set up a large flowerpot and a small one, and try to *point out* the relation of "larger than": a person looking where you point—from one pot to the other—may see "different," "same shape," "side by side," "brick-colored," or even "two, a pair," as readily as "larger than." Relations are abstract, and abstract entities are embodied only in symbols. The profound difference between speech-gifted beings and speechless ones is due to the power of words to set forth relations, which cannot be seen and touched, yet are the bonds among our sensations that create "facts." Our world of facts is shot through and through with concepts comprehended symbolically; "nature" is far more a language-made affair than people generally realize—made not only for sense, but for understanding, and prone to collapse into chaos if ideation fails.

At the center of human experience, then, there is always the activity of imagining reality, conceiving the structure of it through words, images, or other symbols, and assimilating actual perceptions to it as they come— that is, *interpreting* them in the light of general, usually tacit ideas. This process of interpretation is so natural and constant that most of it goes on unconsciously. Instead of having sensations and judging them to "mean" the existence of things or the occurrence of events, we really *perceive things and happenings,* and become directly aware of "facts." The whole intellectual framework of space and time, things and properties, change, cause and effect, and so on, is implicit in the very way we use our senses. The perception of relations, connections, and especially of *meaning* takes place through any and all avenues of sense; this kind of perception is the *logical intuition* contained in human experience as such, the factor that makes it human, different from animal response. It is reflected by the ways people use words (the "syntax" of their particular language), of which there are varieties, but all varieties of syntax serve to formulate *propositions,* and give rise to discourse and discursive reasoning. All our experience—practical, ethical, or intellectual—is built up on an intuitively constructed logical scaffold known as common sense.

As human awareness differs from that of animals, so,

of course, do human feeling and emotion. Since our environment is a world, we have feelings toward the world —not transient excitements, but a permanent emotional attitude toward a permanent "universe." This attitude is the deepest level of feeling in us, by virtue of which we have a continuous emotional life; and, like all human feelings, it is closely related to imagination. It is fed, in each person, by his envisagement of the world, and of human life, and of himself in that frame: that is to say, by his orientation in reality. His experiences may be many or few; so long as they are capable of interpretation in terms of common sense, his knowledge of reality can grow just by adding facts, without changing his world image or disturbing his sense of orientation, which is always the keynote in a coherent life of feeling.

Common sense is the unconscious use of categories and concepts that fit common experience. It has grown up through ages, from the earliest forms of characteristically human perception and reaction that is, the earliest ways of thinking—to what we recognize as sensible, logical thinking today. Its gradual development is reflected in the evolution of languages, a fascinating field of study that has only recently been opened and promises to be rich in new historical and psychological materials. Philosophers, too, have harvested their share of ideas from the linguists' new researches, which coincide with the great work of Frege, Peirce, and Russell on literal symbolism, and of Cassirer on symbolic forms as such, to give present-day philosophy its semantic turn.

The use of words is always an index to people's intellectual power: the vagueness or precision of the distinctions they draw between one thing and another may be seen in their choice of distinct words for those things, or their tendency to let one word serve many purposes and shift its meaning without taking account of relevant differences. The centers of attention are marked by the "key words" in their discourse—nouns in our Indo-European languages, held together by verbs that symbolize our awareness of relations, and elaborated with modifiers to express further distinctions. There are other languages in which actions are named by the "key words" and things are grammatically expressed as conditions of the actions, that is, by modifiers. Societies that differ radically in the logical structure of their languages have really a different inheritance of common sense, and their mutual understanding presents a deeper problem than they themselves realize when they establish a rough vocabulary to serve both parties in commerce with each other. The words of that vocabulary have a core of practical meaning for both, but the connotations that accrue to a word in the course of its career probably tend to grow apart as long as each group continues to live with its own language.

The power of language to keep step with the expansion of human experience through the long course of history lies in the tendency of words to mean more than they designate, or symbolize directly; for they tend to symbolize indirectly *anything for which their direct meaning itself may be a symbol.* The word "light" designates a physical phenomenon we perceive with our eyes, but light itself is a world-old symbol for knowledge, intelligence, reason, logical intuition (John Locke called such intuition "natural light"), and also for a large class of feelings—joy, relief, love, and religious exaltation. All things that light itself commonly symbolizes accrue to the word "light," as its *metaphorical meanings,* so naturally and originally that in studying the history of words it is impossible to judge whether the physical or the emotional or some other meaning is the oldest. Max Müller, a great philologist of the nineteenth century, called the physical meaning the "root metaphor," taking for granted that words originally meant physical objects and physical actions, as they most readily do for our common sense. The truth, however, is probably that in the pristine sense of a word all those conceptions, which we now call its several meanings, were not several, but that they have gradually become separated out of a matrix of vague, great significance, physical and emotional at once, felt rather than understood. Daylight was probably experienced as joy and night as trouble before any primitive thinker realized that light is one thing and joy another, darkness one thing and trouble another, and that light gave him joy and darkness caused him trouble.

The root metaphor is the image conveyed by the word,

and this image may mean a feeling, an act, an object, even a personality or a place. All sorts of things may appear *in this image,* that is, they may *be imagined in this form.* The essence of human mentality is the use of images not as sheer memory traces, but as symbols which may be put together freely, elaborated, and treated as mental pictures of the most various experiences, *i.e.,* the power of seeing one thing in another.

The processes of nature, especially, may be seen one in another; and those which are hard to observe are generally understood only through a model. Death is seen as an eternal sleep, youth and age as spring and autumn or winter, life as a flame consuming the candle that provides it. The very framework of experience is only thinkable by means of models: time is most readily imagined as a flowing stream, and is, in fact, so hard to conceive without that metaphorical image that many people believe time literally flows. Space is usually thought of as a huge vessel that contains all things but could also be empty; the fact that a vessel is necessarily something *in* space, dividing an inside from an outside, does not disturb the naïve imagination. Space is a receptacle, and all matter is in in it.

Because we see one thing in another—life in the candle flame, death in sleep, time in the flowing stream, space in a bowl or in the sky that we see as an inverted bowl —the vast multiplicity of experiences compose one world for us. Our symbolic seeing is what gives that world its fundamental unity, much deeper than the unity of its causal connectedness—the gnomonic "likeness in difference" that unifies a nest of tables, rather than the simple concatenation of links that unifies a chain. Most of the things we encounter have no obvious causal connections: the roar of a passing plane, and the voice from the radio advertising toothpaste, the thermometer at freezing, the dog scratching himself under the table. It is an article of scientific faith (and a primary one) that all events are causally connected, however complex the web of their connections may be. We really see causal connections only in a few chains of events. Something bites the dog, so he scratches; the scratching bothers us, so presently we nudge him; because we nudge him, he stops for a moment and then uses the other leg. That is a causal chain; but so far as our direct observation is concerned, most things "just happen" at the moment when they do, and could have been otherwise. We believe them to have causes, but their causes have to be learned, or taken on faith.

What we do see, however, is that the most various things repeat a few fundamental forms, by virtue of which we can use familiar events as *models* to understand new ones and tangible objects as symbols of intangible realities. This helps a person in two ways to cope with his world: in the first place, by making great and remote parts or aspects of it conceivable, and secondly, by giving its homely, trivial contents a symbolic value. When ordinary acts like eating and sleeping, and common things like fire and trees and water, become symbols for the round of nature, human passion, and what not, they cease to be silly and separate items of experience, and take on significance as integral factors in the human scene.

This import of everyday things, the reflection of a cosmic order in the order of common life, is what builds up a person's world image, the frame in which his beliefs and doubts and judgments all make sense. The possession of such a frame is *mental orientation*. It is usually unrecognized, or only vaguely recognized, but it is the first requisite for a concerted "inner life"; for the sense of general orientation in the world is the basis of our emotional security. Like the pressure of the floor against our feet, it is not normally in consciousness; but let it fail, and we are scarcely conscious of anything else; there is complete disorientation and everything joins the confusion.

The unity of nature is not all that we owe to our power of symbolic thinking, which spontaneously makes conceptual metaphors and models out of sensory objects. Our ideas of moral qualities, good and evil, blessing and bane, seem all to have been attained with the help of concrete imagery, often of a very earthy sort. The expression of values is so consistently metaphorical that words like "high" and "low," "straight" and "crooked," have almost more readily a moral connotation than a geometrical one; it is hard, sometimes, to tell which is their primary sense and which the derivative. Without the concepts they convey we would have no moral world. The same thing holds for our conception of intellectual functions and qualities: "bright" and "dull," "keen," "obscure," "hard," even words like "wit," of which the root metaphor is "white," are obviously physical terms; but without them we could not have developed the characteristically human sense of intellectual and moral existence.

Metaphorical images penetrate deeply into our common-sense ways of thinking. Nobody questions the good sense of saying that a tree spreads its branches in order to catch as much light as possible; the model of a person voluntarily lifting his arms in order to receive something beneficent coming from above is forgotten when we talk about the tree as though *it spread* the branches for *its purpose*. In fact, this guiding image is so forcible that most people who do not believe the tree has insight and intentions and voluntary motions still cannot surrender the metaphor of purposive action entirely; if the tree does not act from choice, some intelligent agent must be *making* it grow one way rather than another, in order that it may catch the scant forest light.

We often oppose what we call "poetic metaphors" to "hard common sense." But common sense is built on poetic metaphors.

Yet common sense is not poetry. The power of seeing one thing in another, which begets our metaphors and conceptual models (the oldest of which are *myths* of nature and human life), leads also to a characteristically human thought process known as abstraction. By logical intuition we see not only what is "the same" in two widely different things, as for instance a burning candle consumed by its flame and a living body consumed by its life, but also what makes them different. As soon as the differences are clearly recognized, the common element stands out against them, and can be conceived alone as that which both of these different things exhibit. In this way the *concept,* e.g., "matter being consumed by its own activity," is abstracted; and a mind which can make such an abstraction realizes that life is not literally a burning candle but is reasonably symbolized by one.

Language registers this logical abstraction in the growth of its vocabulary. The concepts with which we operate in our daily lives—concepts of things and properties, mind and matter, necessity, money value, moral value, good and evil—all may be traced back, through the history of the words that express them, to their origins in vaguer but usually richer "root metaphors." The abstract sense of our words today has been derived by a process of distinction and separation that results in the establishment of at least one literal meaning, and often a number of recognized metaphorical uses. So we may find, for instance: "Bright: giving or reflecting light; figuratively, of quick intelligence." But here the figurative use is so common that most dictionaries today (e.g., Webster's, or Funk & Wagnall's) list it as a second literal meaning.

In discourse and even more in writing we continue to give words new figurative meanings; and as there are many ways of "seeing" a new object or event, there is often a wide choice of older things to which it might be assimilated. Who decided that the covering of an automobile engine was to be called the "hood" in America, and in England, France, and Germany, the "bonnet"? Who called a cover for certain smaller units a "cowl," then made "cowl" a verb and derived the verbal noun "cowling" for the same object? Who called the cover for the hub of the wheel a "cap"? No one knows. All these words denote headgear, the most familiar loose covering for a special part, and the analogy is obvious enough so that we accept the extended meaning without difficulty. A cover fitting closely all around something is usually designated as a "shoe"; again, we find the figure of speech natural, and soon forget it is a figure. By metaphorical extension, "shoe" becomes the literal name of the fitted casings on tires as well as the fitted casings on our feet.

In this way language grows with conception, and usually conception keeps pace with new experiences. The repository of all our concepts, old and new, quite abstract ones and inveterately poetic ones, is common sense, the generally accepted basis of reasonable discourse, knowledge, and good judgment.

But common sense is not a perfect conceptual system,

self-consistent and coherent, by which all of reality could be understood. It is built by a spontaneous imagination that draws on many sources, and the images it employs are often incompatible; so it is really a rough-and-ready instrument that is prone to yield absurdities when its concepts are tested for all they imply. Their implications are often in flat contradiction to each other, or lead to a jumble of bizarre, unrelated beliefs. For instance, people who have studied just a little bit of psychology—say, an introductory course in college—can see by common sense that the concept of "the will," as a distinct faculty or power, is untenable; but in moral and religious debates they continue to worry and argue about "freedom of the will." They cannot drop the traditional common-sense assumption that an entity called "the will" is the real agent behind their acts—not part of the body, but somehow inside it, moving it—although in another context they have seen clearly that this assumption makes no sense.

The fact is that any ambitious and sustained intellectual work soon overstrains the capacities of common sense. As soon as one thinks at all seriously and strenuously about nature, society, mind, truth, or any other big and complex subject, the traditional ways of conceiving it prove to be too muddled to allow any distinctions and definitions that might reveal hidden relations, or make obvious ones intelligible. The thinker, therefore, is confronted by the task of criticizing and correcting, perhaps even rejecting, the accepted images and tacit assumptions and of building up a new, more abstract, more negotiable set of concepts.

Such a systematic critique of common sense is philosophy. As William James said, "The word means only the search for *clearness* where common people do not even suspect that there is any lack of it." Philosophy is the pursuit of meanings. It is not a process of finding new facts; the discovery and generalized statement of facts is science. Philosophizing is a process of making sense out of experience, rather than adding to experience itself as factual learning and experimental investigation do.

"The search for clearness"—that is, indeed, the constant quest to which all the special techniques of philosophy are bent. Those techniques constitute a discipline, anciently known and taught as *logic*. Though the study of logic is old and venerable, its most spectacular advances belong to a fairly recent period, and are still in full swing. In the past, logic was almost entirely devoted to *analyzing* the formal concepts in general use—the abstractions implicit in grammar and syntax and ordinary concatenated discourse. With the growth of so-called "symbolic logic," however, logicians have gained a certain freedom from the influence of language, by using other than the traditional, linguistic forms of saying things—that is, other than the subject-and-predicate forms of positive and negative statements. This departure, which started from the invention of a powerful, quasi-mathematical symbolism, has opened up entirely new fields of logical work; it has turned the intellectual searchlights on the principles of abstraction, the necessity and limits of symbolization, and the possible combinations of abstract concepts in the frame of any symbolic system at all, not only what is commonly called a "language." Logical work today, therefore, is more than a matter of analyzing given forms; it consists largely of manipulating odd-looking abstract terms in new combinations, *constructing new formal concepts*.

Clearness, then, is not all that philosophical thinking yields, though that is its constant aim. Concepts may be clear but still inadequate. Suppose we could define to the point of perfect clarity the concept of "phlogiston"; if there is nothing in the world that exemplifies the concept, nothing that fits the definition, or if we cannot combine that concept with any others, its clarity is of no use; we still can do nothing with the term. Concepts must be not only clear but fit for some intellectual purpose. That is the core of truth in the doctrine known as "pragmatism," which asserts that beliefs are true if they "work." It is not the beliefs that are true, but the concepts involved in the beliefs that are *valid,* if—and only if—they work.

Some of the abstractions made by common sense might be made fairly precise and consistent; indeed, that is exactly what begot Euclid's geometry and Aristotle's logic, physics, and psychology. But as observation becomes wider and sharper, and facts pile up on facts, even a refined and codified version of our natural metaphors is not adequate to the growing task of understanding scientific connections. Concepts that begin in concrete images are too simple for the purpose.

At such times, the leaders of human thought do philosophical work. That is why great periods of philosophy follow on periods of fast cultural growth or novel experience: the achievements of Democritus, Socrates, Plato, and Aristotle, on the rise of Greek civilization that culminated in the Age of Pericles, just before their day; medieval philosophy, from Erigena to Aquinas, after the tremendous advent of Christianity; the so-called "modern philosophers"—Descartes, Bacon, and Hobbes, and all their intellectual progeny, slowly dwindling since the giant Kant—in the wake of the Renaissance, to master its welter of discoveries, adventures, and creative outbursts. A high philosophical period marks a stretching of the human mind, a more or less general reorientation in the world, and a new development in men's feeling for nature and for each other.

Such intellectual revolutions begin, of course, where higher abstractions and more negotiable concepts than those of current common sense are needed: among theologians, lawyers, mathematicians, astronomers, physicists, chemists, doctors, biologists, and other professional people dealing with intricate systems of facts or ideas. Experts as well as laymen, when they handle a purely conceptual subject like law or mathematics, invisible materials like those of theology, infinitesimal objects such as "atoms" and even parts of atoms, or inaccessible portions of the world, as one does in astronomy, necessarily resort to a model, i.e., a symbolic image taken from more familiar experience to represent an elusive concept. A scientist will demonstrate to himself and others the action of a heart by means of a simply constructed pump, with four valves and two loops of hose; or he will let a construction of metal rods and balls represent the tiny distances, and other relations, among whirling particles of electrically charged matter called "protons" and "electrons," assumed to compose the submicroscopic material elements which today bear the name of "atoms."

When the conceptual frame of our thinking is inadequate for understanding our world, the models that have served it in the past will not do any more. The first theory of atoms was propounded more than two thousand years ago, by the Greek philosopher Democritus; [1] his illustrations of the way atoms composed matter were taken from the sands of the sea, hard bits of stone settling by their weight into large masses, and from dust motes seen in sunbeams, exhibiting constant motion that he thought was "of their nature." His conception of atoms involved shape and motion, but not any inside structure or parts. In fact, the name he gave his material elements, "atoms," means "indivisible," i.e., without parts. Atomic structure, as we know it, could not be thought of without a new concept, or rather a whole set of new concepts —electromagnetic force, positive and negative charge, units of energy, and several other terms of analysis that were not current and, indeed, not possible in his day. Philosophical thinking had not reached the level of abstraction to which they belong.

Because we do operate with such notions, the old Greek models of physical substance are no good to us any more. Our philosophy of nature has outgrown them, and scientific observation shows us conditions they cannot represent. The chief reason, however, why physicists were never content with the ancient concept of the atom was that this concept harbored a logical inconsistency. A simple substance, such as Democritus assumed, has really no properties except those of spatial extension. No matter how small such extension may be, it is never indivisible. One can imagine a particle of solid matter being indivisible in practice, that is, because we have no instrument that will further divide it; but in theory the end of its divisiblity cannot be established at any magnitude.

This is a typical instance of the sort of conceptual problem that arises in science, religion, politics, or any other field of systematic interest, and presents a philo-

[1] Or, probably, his teacher Leucippus; but the Latin poet Lucretius, from whom we have it, associates it for us with the name of Democritus.

sophical challenge. It is not enough to analyze the traditional concept, find it logically untenable, and reject the word "atom" as meaningless; "atom" does mean something that exists, but what answers to it in actuality cannot be a particle of absolutely hard matter, like an infinitesimal stone. At this point we have to construct a new meaning, one that will bear logical analysis and permit us still to use the word "atom" in describing the different forms of physical substance. This is the constructive work of philosophy. It is by far the greater part of that discipline; analysis shapes the problem and serves as a constant check, but logical construction is its real life. It requires imagination, skill in manipulating formal definitions, and above all a certain boldness and freedom of mind to depart from traditional ways of thinking and talking, dispense with the old misleading models, and even dismiss the promptings of common sense with lordly unconcern in the interest of abstract conceivability.

Ordinarily, in a normal and settled society, the limitations of common sense are of little concern to the average person. Even its paradoxes and absurdities do not disturb him, for he is not aware of them. The frame of his thinking, and therewith of his actions, passions, expectations, and all the business of his life, is rough but firm. It is chiefly a fabric of images taken from the most familiar aspects of existence: the space of his own living extended to larger and larger proportions is the space of his universe; years—measured by the turns of the earth about its axis—stretch into his own past and beyond it, and into his future and beyond it, to make eternity. From his social experience he borrows the image of an imposed law regulating people's actions, and does not even know he is creating a metaphor when he calls the regularities of nature "natural law"; and as an authority imposes laws on people, he can hardly elude the assumption of a vastly greater authority imposing an absolute and perfect law on things, which consequently "obey" natural law in every point.

In times of rapid changes, however, when society is neither normal nor settled, the average person is driven to thinking about things beyond his own round of life— things that uphold this essential round, and suddenly seem insecure: providence and its plan, the credentials of human authorities, the validity of morals and institutions, the value or vanity of work and of life itself.

Few men can think through such problems to a point of decision, any more than they could think out for themselves the reasons for expecting an eclipse on the fifth of next month at ten o'clock. But their mental security is not necessarily disturbed by this fact, so long as they believe implicitly that the major issues of life *can be understood* by those who really put their minds wholly to the task—that is, that there are answers, and human reason can shape them. That is the chief importance of the professional philosopher for the layman—the reason why Plato's doctrine of ideas and Aristotle's teleology mattered to the merchants and soldiers of Greece, who had heard of them only vaguely if at all; why the *Summa theologica* of St. Thomas was of vast importance to all Christendom, though probably only the higher clergy read it, and only in the Western church at that; and why, in the heyday of an expanding secular culture following the Renaissance, in a new world of science and modern commerce, Locke's *Essay on Human Understanding* was an intellectual bombshell, and Newton's *Principia mathematica,* written in Latin and consisting largely of mathematical statements, intellectually affected people who were neither scientists nor mathematicians and had never studied a page of it.

Trained and specialized thinking is always in the vanguard of our conceptual development; what is abstruse and weird to one generation is usually quite acceptable to the next. It is the same in philosophy as in art and music: what we find comprehensible, the painting of El Greco or the music of Beethoven, was once received with reluctance or even violent protest as distorted modern stuff. John Locke had to plead against people's common-sense beliefs when he argued that the source of all our factual knowledge is sensation (that notion was old, but not popularly known); Kant, a hundred years later, had to fly in the face of common sense to call the same doctrine in question. Abstractly and logically developed concepts seep down into untutored thought only as concrete, familiar models are found to picture them. They seem reasonable to the average person just in so far as they are imaginable. And usually the advance of knowledge is slow enough to let such popular versions of new concepts take shape.

It is, after all, imagination that frames and supports and guides our thinking, not only about the practicalities of the day, but also about much greater things—good and evil, love, life and death, past and future, and human destiny. The average person probably does not contemplate such matters very often, but he has ideas about them, as we say, "at the back of his head"—gathered since childhood, from church, from impressive moments, and in sleepless nights. When he does have occasion to face fundamental issues of moral principle, hope or renunciation, self or society, the terms in which he thinks must make some clear sense to him; it is here that he needs a definite and adequately big world image.

We live, today, in an anxious world. Later generations will probably see our age as a time of transition from one social order to another, as we find the Middle Ages a "middle" between the Graeco-Roman civilization and the full-fledged European. But we cannot see the present that way, because what we are moving toward does not yet exist, and we can have no picture of it. Nor is the ascendancy of Europe—the concert of nations consisting of white people, and their economic culture roughly coextensive with Christendom—as yet a finished act in history; but its form is broken. We feel ourselves swept along in a violent passage, from a world we cannot salvage to one we cannot see; and most people are afraid.

The deluge of novel experience that has overtaken us in the past two or three generations is, of course, widely recognized as the source of our general disorientation. Everybody knows how the social, economic, and physical aspects of life have changed—how artisan labor has given place to machinery, how new modes of travel and communication have revolutionized the social structure, bringing the most primitive cultures into direct contact with the most civilized, and how modern war and modern commerce, being worldwide, have mixed up all races and religions and tongues in a bedlam of fantastic adventure. These facts need no reiteration.

What few people realize is that the changed and still-changing conditions of life are only one thing—the most tangible thing—that keeps us in a state of nervous tension verging on hysteria. There is a deeper source of anxiety, below the level of practical expectations and even of explicit thought: that is the growing inadequacy of words, and especially certain key words which have always functioned in our moral and political discourse, to express exactly what we mean in such discourse to-day. Perhaps the present popular excitement about "semantics" springs from a half-baked, but essentially sound, awareness of this profoundest trouble. It is a curious fact that really important philosophical issues usually evoke some echo from the public mind; indeed, the public at large has an uncanny way of feeling the importance of things about which it knows nothing explicitly. But cults and their campaigns—such as teaching huge audiences the first, superficial, often specious findings of semantic research—are quack medicine for grave philosophical ills. The inadequacy of words points to a more serious difficulty than the emotive use of language, and to get away from Aristotelian categories of thought requires more than a new formula which can be learned. The diagnosis may be essentially right, but the cure is an attack on symptoms.

What those symptoms reveal is a general frustration of our conceptual powers in the face of the new world, and that means, of course, inability to reason clearly about it; consequently we lack theoretical foundations to support any assertion about the things that concern us most urgently—human rights, loyalty, freedom, democracy, religion, nationality, culture. The cause of this bankruptcy lies in two conditions: the speed with which practical changes have overtaken the world, and the sudden expansion of thought. Both actual life and theoretical thinking have outrun our powers of imagination; so the average person—simple or sophisticated—is unable to picture the universe, or even to conceive what the near future is likely to be. The world image has collapsed.

Our chief disconcertment stems not from new experiences, but from the fact that space and time, the implicit framework of all experience, have changed; history actually unfolds faster than it has ever done in the past. The development of political events is directly influenced by the speed of communication and travel. Consider, for instance, the difference between the Roman wars with the Goths and with the Huns, respectively. The Goths migrated with their families, slowly pushing their westward frontier, always threatening the established empire of Rome. When the Caesar moved against them, the danger was obvious, but the crisis—the actual invasion of Italy, the first march on the city—was still far in the offing. The Goths moved at the leisurely pace of loaded wagons and of families walking, and the political situation changed at the same rate. The Huns came with the speed of riding men. The news of their coming could scarcely precede them, for it could fly only at a messenger's stretched gallop. Almost as soon as Rome knew it, the Hun was at the gate. The political crisis was immediate.

Our history has speeded up at the rate of our communication and travel, which is so accelerated that we can no longer conceive it as "twice as fast," "ten times as fast," as older ways. It is just out of all proportion, so that our old standards cannot even be modified to take the new measurements. Now matter how carefully we tell ourselves that things happen faster today than they used to, our ideas of them still lag behind the change. This gives all current history an air of extraordinary pressure, like a sudden emergency. The late Franklin D. Roosevelt said, "You can't have an emergency for thirty years." True enough; but you can have a *sense* of emergency as long as that and longer.

Space, too, has undergone fundamental changes, not only in the realm of astronomy but in our earthly reckonings. Ever since the invention of steam power and the even more revolutionary gasoline motor, distances have been shrinking, as everyone knows. But recently something more radical than that has happened to the space of our living: the physical nature of places has changed. With the advent of air travel, our paths that used to be bound to the earth's topology now lie level in the upper air, and natural barriers—mountains, canyons, rivers, ice-caps, and oceans—have lost their old meanings. Only the highest ranges present a "hump" in the space of our travel. The startling result is that *the earth has no secluded places any more.* Deep valleys and jungle-girded retreats lie open to peering eyes as they do to the sky. There are no more hiding places. Neither are there any real natural fastnesses; the old strongholds on cliffs and peaks are only the easier targets.

At the same time, scientific thinking, which in Newton's day was just gaining the status of "common sense" and displacing the more poetic, religious mode of thought of former centuries, has not stopped in its development. Kepler, Galileo, and Newton were only a beginning. Scientific conception has grown like Jack's beanstalk ever since, and soon left the vivid popular imagination behind. Modern mathematical operations are entirely alien to any metaphorical images we can muster. Yet we know something of this great mental adventure, for in civilized societies today almost everyone can read, and the radio spreads new ideas even to circles where reading is not commonly practiced, so that everyone learns of what is going on, and the biggest thing going on is science. Our imagination is influenced by scientific notions that our reason cannot really fathom, especially since the most exciting ones have probably passed through the radio as through the meat chopper.

The result is that the most advanced and thrilling thought of our day moves in a realm of its own. Its results come to us in the guise of "science wonders," "miracle drugs," and comic-book nightmares of interstellar wars or world-consuming explosions started by a mislaid grain of dust. The theoretical constructions behind the wonders transcend the very language we speak; they can be expressed only in mathematical symbols.

But the genuine scientific notions that have gradually become embodied in popular thought are straining it in another way: some of our most important ethical symbols have lost much if not all of their power. "High" and "low" have always symbolized good and evil; "up" and "down" therefore designated moral direction as well as spatial. The realization that "above" and "below" do not indicate fixed places, that the daytime sky and the night sky are different parts of space, and "up" and "down" mean, respectively, "away from the earth's center" and "toward the earth's center," has subtly, but profoundly influenced moral thought; for as the literal meanings of terms like "up" and "down" are seen to be relative, and what is more, relative to the earth, their symbolic sense, too, ceases to appear as something absolute, and implies a terrestrial point of origin.

This is only one example, but others are not hard to find. Religion has always drawn on the model of patriarchal government, raised to the glorious degree of a monarch who owned his realm and all his subjects, a Pharaoh, a Solomon, a Caesar, a Louis. In an age that resents dynastic rule and extols democracy, the divine ruler no longer appears in the image of something we admire, but in that of an obsolete personage or else a fairytale king. Except in a few countries that have not yielded yet to the prevailing trend, the once wise, omnipotent, and above all splendid king today is hedged about by restrictions of his power and checks on his wisdom, and walks in the garb of a somewhat formal and precise man of affairs. Earthly government is no longer a "natural symbol" of the cosmic rule once conceived in its image.

The old metaphors have lost their aptness, the old models are broken, and humanity—especially the most sensitive and thoughtful part of humanity everywhere—has lost its mental orientation and moral certitude.

Philosophy today shows violent symptoms of this intellectual collapse. Its most important exhibit is the tendency of serious present-day thinkers to base their whole philosophical undertaking not on human rationality, but on despair of reason. This makes philosophy itself not a process of constructing logical foundations for science, art, religion, and human relations, but a disciplining of the mind to accept unreason, a daily and hourly *act of will* to eschew reason and live either by faith or by some elected yet absolute "moral commitment." This attitude, rather than any doctrine, is the spirit of "existentialism" which pervades most of contemporary philosophy and literature in continental Europe, and to some extent in the English-speaking countries too.

The tenets that unite the several philosophers who

call themselves "existentialists"—notably Heidegger and Jaspers in Germany,[2] Sartre and Marcel in France—are programmatic rather than doctrinal. In doctrine these writers are often far apart. It is in aim, starting point, and method that they belong to one spiritual movement.

Their starting point is the recognition of *existence* as an ultimate inward experience—not only one's own existence, but that of the world, which has the same character. Their problem is not to understand existence, because it is essentially irrational and therefore eludes understanding, but to accept and appreciate it. The deeper motivation of their quest is to *put* values into the world where they do not *find* them.

This is not an uncommon motive at any time, and in an age of cultural transition, full of tension, paradox, and uncertainty, it is a powerful one; it turns thousands of people from their own vain efforts to cope with the world into the folds of religious faiths. But most people have little to sacrifice in this exchange; these men, quite otherwise, cannot easily rid themselves of their own reason that revolts against absurdity. Their writings are full of rational ideas and able arguments. Such thinkers find the acceptance of contradictions a heavy task. They have the temptation of rationality to contend with; and their philosophic method, therefore, demands a constant humiliation of reason. This humiliation is the free moral act, the *constant choice,* which the existentialist has to practice as the simple religious zealot practices constant prayer.

The promise of existentialism is individual selfhood, reorientation, the rescue of an emotional life that was disconcerted by fear of chaos, nothingness, and alienation. Its progress is a biographical one. The aim of this whole philosophical venture is to transcend personal limitations, meet personal needs, and solve personal problems, no matter how many persons have the same

---

2 Both of these writers have lately repudiated the existentialist movement, as every active philosopher must reject a label that lumps his ideas with other people's. Though he was the founder of the school that bears it, Peirce rejected the label "pragmatist" after James published the "pragmatist theory of truth." Historically, Heidegger and Jaspers have been leaders of the existentialist movement, as Peirce was of the pragmatist.

anxiety to allay and the same "inwardness" to achieve. In this respect it resembles the ancient Hellenistic schools of Stoics, Cynics, Epicureans, and Cyrenaics; and like them, it does not contribute to theoretical thinking, because it is not a theory but an experience. It begins in "fear and trembling" and culminates in transcendence, or freedom, or affirmation of God, or self-realization in death, but not in any advance of thought; for thought is said only to build up paradoxes.

Existentialism is a movement of intellectual retreat. There may be wisdom in retreat, but at the present time there is, above all, grave danger in it. If the leaders of thought, the philosophers by vocation and training, despair of reason, who will maintain the nerve of all knowledge that it may stretch its reaches to keep the terrifying accretion of new facts in its command?

There are, fortunately, people philosophizing today who are not so consciously disoriented that the solution of personal problems dominates their systematic thought. They see philosophy as a critique of working concepts in all domains of life, especially those where old concepts are obsolete and new ones still incoherent and perhaps more than a little metaphorical. Paradox, which the existentialists regard as the end of all rational argument, is to these more extrovert thinkers its starting point, not its stopping place. Paradoxical ideas are imperfectly formulated ideas, and the philosopher's work is to analyze them, weigh what essential and unessential notions have gone into them (as in the classical idea of *matter* the concept of *mass* is essential, but that of *unconsciousness* or of *ethical worthlessness* is not), and define them without inconsistency. Their definition may sound strange to common sense, but at least it makes sense; and if it is adequate as well as self-consistent, then in another century or less it will even make common sense.

The most alluring, wide-open fields for such new logical work at present are the natural sciences. Scientific concepts have sprung up like mushrooms in the realms of physics, chemistry, astronomy, biology. They have grown not only ahead of popular imagination, but ahead of all current academic philosophy. Great men of science have been their own philosophers. They are never afraid of ideas. Newton, Faraday, Einstein, Planck, and their peers —generation after generation—have invented the new concepts of physical science as they needed them. But of course they have limited their intellectual constructions to the requirements of their subject. Whether these bold abstractions can ever be squared with the economic, legal, moral, aesthetic, and other forms of ideation that obtain in the rest of life is none of the physicist's concern; he is too busy in his own domain to play the metaphysician beyond it, and indeed, whenever he does so his imagination is as unguided by strict problems as anybody's, and is apt to lapse into traditional channels as soon as he ventures on foreign ground. Philosophy has its outposts in every special field, but its frontal advance is a task for its own scholars.

Establishing the rational foundations of scientific propositions is the work that engages the strongest philosophic minds today. It has taken them far into semantic problems: the effect of symbolic forms on meanings, the limits of logical systems, and the grounds for choice of systems. It has started a penetrating analysis of such concepts as space-time, measurement, simultaneity, location, equivalence, structure, dynamic pattern, element, form and function; but this analytic work is interwoven with the processes of new construction and logical imagination, which are naturally called for where sheer analysis can only reveal puzzles and paradoxes. Morton White, editing an anthology of recent philosophical writings, entitled the book *The Age of Analysis*. That designation of our age may be fair. Analyzing concepts is our only formal technique; but few philosophers realize that their analyses are "loaded" with constructive intent, directed toward the formulation of new ideas in terms of which the scientific universe can be made conceivable again as a *world,* engendering and enclosing all things that are real to us.

While the sciences are striding along in seven-league boots, our social thinking seems to be stuck in a quagmire. Its very aims have become problematical. The development of practically limitless physical power has distorted and disrupted the traditional order of world power politics, which was founded on much smaller measures of violence and its effects. As Einstein once remarked, now that we know we can destroy anything we want to destroy, the threat of hostile destruction becomes something extravagant. Since the invention of atomic weapons, armed attack is no longer a reasonable diplomatic trump. A new political order, suited to a worldwide economic system and an essentially footloose, mingling world population, must be in the making, but so far we have no picture of it. If our old ideals and practices have become unreasonable, then unreasonable they are, but we still have them.

We are faced with an unintended, unguided, but irresistible revolution in all human relations, from the marriage bonds and family controls whereby personal life has traditionally been ordered, to the religious and patriotic loyalties that were wont to rule people's wider activities. Such a radical change in the human scene requires and effects a change in the concepts with which we operate practically and intellectually, but few people realize that their basic social conceptions have changed. While our profoundest metaphors have lost their moral import, something equally disconcerting has happened to almost all the strictly literal terms of social theory: they have become equivocal, for they no longer apply to the things we once applied them to, and the shift from old to new applications has shaken their exact sense. When we speak of "community," "society," "democracy," "freedom," we do not mean what our predecessors meant by those terms, but we still say the things they said. A "community" used to mean a more or less permanent group of individuals or families having special relations to each other that they did not have to families or persons outside the group. Can that notion be simply extended to humanity as a whole, the "world community"? "Freedom" used to mean freedom to act without restriction, as one saw fit, and take the consequences; do we mean anything like what the American pioneers called "freedom" when we propose to give people "freedom from want" or "freedom from fear"?

As space and time have changed their appearance and shaken our most elementary footholds in the physical world, language has changed its meanings without our knowing it, and thrown our literal, theoretical discourse into confusion. Our moral and political thinking lacks any sort of conceptual framework of its own. Even in special fields that we dignify with scientific-sounding names—sociology, social psychology, social dynamics—there is no conceptual basis of powerful abstractions to implement deeper and deeper analysis, definitions that can be built up one on another, like the definitions of mathematical terms or physical elements, and the building up of a highly articulated system of relationships. The terminology used at present in so-called "social science" is consciously artificial, but the concepts are still those of common sense, generalized but not abstract: that is to say, they are still prescientific.

As long as political affairs, morals apart from church doctrines, and social issues have no background of coherent, formal thought to which we can take recourse when problems become complicated, "social science" can be no guide to reasonable action. Where there is no theory there is no science, political or social or any other sort.

The usual explanation offered in excuse for this intellectual failure is that precise concepts are impossible and useless in political thought, because people are moved by self-interest or by emotion in politics, and do not act on grounds of reason. That is like saying that engineering can't build a power dam, because dams are built by money and lobbies, not by mathematics. People are just as emotional in religion as in politics; this does not mean that theology must be unsystematic and confused. Engineering does not raise the money or pass the needed bills to get a power dam built, but it does determine, precisely and clearly, what is involved in building the dam whenever we may decide to do so.

We need powerful concepts to cope with the welter of new conditions that beset us. At just this point, conception fails us; we have shifted too many old words to new applications, which their strict literal meanings don't quite fit, to know what we are talking about. So the bottom has gone out of our hard practical thinking. That causes the panic of distrust in reason, or, not uncommonly, a nostalgic desire to return to doctrines rationally and suitably built up in the smaller frame of a more stable world before reason became confused. Then one hears the watchwords: "Back to Kant!" "Back to St. Thomas!" "Back to Aristotle, Plato, Pythagoras!"

But we cannot go backward, except in dream. History moves forward, not backward.

Philosophy must go forward—boldly, over all obstacles —to make language adequate and literal thinking possible and effectual again. In those realms where theory is weakest, and where the terms of discourse are fuzziest, there is the greatest, most urgent work to be done. We must construct the morality of a new age, a new world, and that means a new morality. This cannot be done by adopting some simple new idea and making an "ism" of it—humanism, existentialism, Freudianism—and setting up a few general principles by which all familiar ethical rules are henceforth to be measured. It can only be done by analyzing and perhaps redefining not only obvious ethical aspects of life, but the nature of life itself, and individual life, and mentality, society, and many other subjects. Only in such long and free reflection may the abstract concepts emerge that will make social thinking as vital as physical science, and as mighty. Only by such unremitting work may we hope to engender "social sciences."

The problem of restoring the mental balance which humanity has obviously lost in this age is not psychiatric, or religious, or pedagogical, but philosophical. It is the inadequacy of our concepts that has finally caused all ethical and political thought to break down into rampant ideologies. The only antidote to ideology is active, purposive, confident ideation: that is the philosopher's work.

What we need today is not primarily a rebirth of good will, or a return to some ancient order of life; we need a generation of vigorous thinkers, fiercely devoted to philosophy, trained in logic, linguistics, mathematics, and prepared to learn whatever special skill or knowledge they may find needful on their way—trained as fully as any scientists, without evasion of dry subjects or stepwise procedures—people who can tackle terrible questions and fight through all the misconceptions and confusing traditions that mix up our thoughts and our lives. We must construct the scaffold for our new life, fast, ingeniously, and on big lines. We need big ideas, abstract, powerful, novel—in short, modern—so that the human mind shall always encompass and control what human hands may reach.

INDEX